# Secret Underground Bristol

## Sally Watson

| | |
|---|---|
| Design | **Martin St Amant** |
| Maps and Illustrations | **Lorna Rankin** |
| Original Photography | **Chris Merrick**<br>**Martin St Amant**<br>**Stephen Morris**<br>**Duncan Burgess**<br>**Sarah English** |

**Broadcast Books**

First published by the Bristol
Junior Chamber in 1991.
This edition published October
2002 by Broadcast Books,
4 Cotham Vale, Bristol BS6 6HR.

Cover photograph of Redcliffe Caves by Chris Merrick.

Printed in Great Britain by The Bath Press, Lower
Bristol Road, Bath.

ISBN 1  874092  95  8

We gratefully acknowledge permission to use
photographs and illustrations from

Bath and North East Somerset Council
Bristol City Council
Bristol Industrial Museum
City of Bristol Museum and Art Gallery
City of Bristol Records Office
City of Bristol Reference Library
Peter Davey Collection
Oliver Deardon
Imperial War Museum
Nick McCamley
Managing Trustees of Wesley Chapel, London
Memories
Doug Northcott
Prior Park College
Temple Local History Group
Wessex Water
Sir George White

*This book is dedicated to the memory of*
**Chris Merrick**, *the talented young*
*photographer who was a key member*
*of the team behind the original*
*Secret Underground Bristol.*
*His stunning photographs appear on*
*the cover and several inside pages of*
*this new edition. Chris died in 1998,*
*and he is remembered with great*
*affection by everyone who knew him.*

# Foreword

*F*or over thirty years I've lived a life of ignorance. Countless times I've walked past Bristol's profusion of caves, cellars, grottoes and conduits, and never noticed them. Under my ignorant feet ancient tunnels have twisted and turned. A complete subterranean history lay unheeded beneath my tread.

Archaeologists are usually pretty sceptical about tunnels and secret passages. On virtually every Time Team dig, members of the public approach us, eyes blazing with excitement, to tell us of a long-forgotten passageway somewhere in the locality. We nod and smile but once they've gone, we give a world-weary sigh. Then someone says: "But there'll be nothing there. There never is."

Sally Watson's work gives the lie to such scepticism. Bristol is a veritable Swiss cheese of secret holes. Under Dame Emily Playpark, where my daughter learned to roller skate, there's a huge pit shaft, five times deeper than the Avon Gorge. Below Pen Park Road, where my son played primary school football, lies an immense natural cavern. Bristolians will be amazed by the proximity of this profusion of long-lost labyrinths. Visitors will discover a Bristol that's virtually unknown, even to its residents. Whoever you are, dip in and discover the treasures that lie deep down below our great city.

Tony Robinson

# Contents

# Introduction

If you think you are standing on solid ground, think again. Beneath your feet is another Bristol—a hidden city of tunnels and waterways, caves and grottoes, cellars and sewers, with a secretive life of its own.

The Bristol Junior Chamber—which is well-known for initiating imaginative projects such as the Balloon Fiesta—decided to explore this subterranean city back in the early 1990s. Together with Sally Watson, a professional writer and archaeologist, we unearthed an amazing underworld and hundreds of fascinating stories. The result was the first edition of *Secret Underground Bristol*—which rapidly became the most popular book ever written about the City.

After a few years, the 1991 edition became somewhat out-of-date and we decided not to reprint—but readers have continually demanded the return of *Secret Underground Bristol*. We have now prepared a completely new edition—updated, extended and with three times more colour photographs and illustrations than the original. It includes many discoveries made by readers, and has been expanded to take in exciting underground features beyond the City boundaries.

*Secret Underground Bristol* takes you on an exhilarating voyage through the City's eerie underworld—but there are still many mysteries to discover, and the search continues…

The Bristol Junior Chamber is a dynamic group of young professional and business people, promoting the business and cultural life of Bristol. To find out more, log on to:

www.bristoljuniorchamber.co.uk

# A very pleasant

According to Daniel Defoe, eighteenth-century Bristolians were a money-grabbing lot with "souls engrossed with lucre". On the surface, he was right. Then, as now, Bristol's business people were hard-headed folk—but there was more to them than that. If Defoe had dug a little deeper, he would have unearthed closet romantics, living out their fantasies in weird underground grottoes.

A grotto is the strangest of all follies—an artificial cave. Building these hidden retreats seems to have been particularly appealing to secretive Bristolians. It is surely no accident that, out of the handful of British grottoes which have survived, Bristol boasts two extraordinary examples. In Clifton, there is one of the oldest, finest and most famous in the country; in Warmley, one of the least-known and most mysterious. Both were built in the eighteenth century—the heyday of the folly. Georgian gentlefolk were infatuated with the picturesque, and

*Goldney Hall grounds: the figure in red is standing by the entrance to the Grotto*

# place—for a toad

a mournful ruin added immeasurably to a carefully contrived "natural" landscape. England became littered with grottoes, sham castles, pointless columns, Gothic towers and even a mock Stonehenge. The most ambitious folly-builders included ornamental humans in their schemes. Hermits were in great demand for grottoes and sanctuaries, and there seems to have been no shortage. Recruitment advertisments produced a healthy response, despite the fact that average conditions of employment included living underground without speaking, shaving or nail-clipping for a full seven years. The rewards were high for any hermit who stuck it out until the end of that mystic term, but many fell by the wayside. One exasperated employer suffered such a high turnover that he was forced to use a stuffed hermit.

Alexander Pope, who built the first true grotto in the garden of his Twickenham home in the 1720s, never had to resort to such expedients. Being a diminutive hunch-back and a famous poet into the bargain,

*The entrance to Goldney's magical underworld*

*Details from Goldney Grotto.*      **Above: the pool**      **Right: shellwork**

he was as colourful a character as any grotto could hope to entertain. Pope aimed for the natural look in his underground retreat, the better to commune with Nature and his Muse. His grotto was rough and irregular like a real cave, and was decorated with stalactites which friends had shot down like partridge in Cheddar Caves. According to Dr. Johnson, Pope "adorned it with fossile bodies, and dignified it with the title of grotto, a place of silence and retreat, from which he endeavoured to persuade his friends and himself that cares and passions could be excluded." Unimpressed

by either the place or its undersized owner, Johnson concluded that "a grotto is a very pleasant place—for a toad!".

Nevertheless, Pope's grotto was much celebrated at the time, and probably inspired Thomas Goldney III to build an underground extravaganza in the grounds of his Clifton mansion. Happily, this superb grotto is beautifully preserved in the gardens of Goldney House (now a University Hall of Residence) and can be viewed on occasional Open Days.

The entrance to the grotto is a Gothic façade built into the side of a hill. It looks innocuous enough, but passing through it

is unnerving. From the civilised world of trim lawns and afternoon tea, you are suddenly plunged into a pagan underworld. Everything is bathed in the eerie green glow of moss-laden skylights, and echoes to the crash of water. The cavern is gloomy and glistening at the same time— encrusted with thousands of shells, conches, crystals, fossils and corals like the cave of some eccentric water god. You turn instinctively left, towards the sound of water—and there he is. Far away, it seems, at the top of a narrow cleft, lounges a marble deity. From the urn at his right hand, water cascades down over the rocks, singing through the shells, and tumbles into a deep pool at your feet. As your eyes grow accustomed to the light, you see that the grotto has other strange occupants. At the back of the main chamber, a plaster-of-Paris lion glares sightlessly at you as he guards the den in which his mate crouches. From the western end of the grotto, several tunnels branch off. One is 100 feet/30 metres long and emerges at the other side of the garden. Perhaps Goldney brought visitors down this way at night, so that the candle-lit grotto would take their breath away after a long, dark walk. Another tunnel leads up behind the cascade, past the god's cave and into the bottom of Goldney Tower.

This was built to house a steam engine which pumped water to the grotto's cascade and to the fountains in the lily pond (nowadays, this is done by electricity).

*Left and above: the Goldney Water God*

commissioned and the cascade to be engineered. It is said that Goldney employed men for seven years to collect the "Bristol Diamonds" which encrust the pillars supporting the roof of the cavern. The grotto was clearly a labour of love. It is also unique, and seems to have sprung almost entirely from the imagination of its creator. Once Pope had set the trend, grottoes did become very fashionable, but most builders copied standard models from pattern books. Goldney does not appear to have copied anything. His grotto is one of the earliest in Britain, and it is far more complex than any started at a similar date. When Mrs. Mary Delaney, a society grotto-designer of repute, saw it in 1756 she declared that it was "by much the finest thing of the kind I ever saw". We can probably take her word for it. This resourceful lady once contrived to turn her ballroom into a forest, complete with a grotto and a Gothic chapel which doubled as a sideboard—so if anyone knew their way around a folly, it was she.

*The Goldney lioness guards her lair*

Thomas Goldney III expended 27 long years of effort (from 1737 to 1764) on his grotto. The outline of the main chamber was in place by August 1739 (the date is picked out in shells on the rooflight of the west hall), but there were still innumerable shells and fossils from all over the world to be collected, statuary to be

*Entrance to Goldney Grotto*

philosopher but a hard-working, Quaker banker and businessman. Again, Mrs. Delaney may offer a clue. "The master", she says, "is reckoned a great humorist". Perhaps the eccentric bachelor just wanted to amaze and amuse. Unlike Pope's gloomy den, Goldney's theatrical grotto is designed not so much for quiet contemplation as for gasps of astonishment and delicious chills down the spine.

The great humorist no doubt delighted in the amazement of his friends. The grotto also helped to raise his social standing by attracting well-connected visitors. This may have been a strong motivation for Goldney, whose family was far from aristocratic and had not always been entirely respectable. His grandfather (Thomas Goldney I) was a grocer, albeit a prosperous one, and a staunch Quaker. His son, Thomas Goldney II, was a more adventurous

Why Goldney spent so much time and money on his grotto, and what he did in it, are far from clear. He was not a poet or

*Goldney Tower, which housed the steam engine that powered the cascade in the Grotto*

*The Goldney Lion*

businessman but somewhat less devout. He built up the family fortunes and acquired the estate in Clifton, but not without sacrificing some of his Quaker principles. He had several legitimate interests, such as financing Abraham Darby's pioneering iron works, but in 1708 he sponsored a privateering voyage designed to capitalise on the war with France. The Society of Friends was deeply disturbed, but there was little they could do about it. Goldney was in prison for suspected fraud at the time.

So when Thomas Goldney III became head of the family in 1731 at the age of 35, he was secure financially but there was a good deal of ground to make up socially. As his father had already rebuilt the family home, he set about enlarging the estate and laying out superb gardens, complete with that most aristocratic of extravagances—a folly. If Goldney wanted

to establish himself as a real gentleman, there was no better way to do it.

This still does not fully explain why the folly he chose was a grotto. The spectacular, open views from his grounds would have provided the perfect setting for a classical temple or Gothic ruin, and he could have run one up in a tenth of the time. There must be a more personal and emotional reason behind the grotto. Perhaps Goldney simply longed for adventure. In the days of his maverick father, he had had a taste of it. That scandalous privateering voyage, which returned when Goldney was 15, brought back one particularly spectacular find— Alexander Selkirk, the castaway who inspired Defoe's *Robinson Crusoe*. The Captain also collected gorgeous Pacific shells and corals which he presented to his sponsor's son—together with exciting travellers' tales, no doubt. All this must surely have made a tremendous impression on an imaginative youth like Goldney. He certainly developed a taste for the exotic if his library—which included a *Life of Mahomet* and *The Arabian Nights*—is anything to go by. Perhaps, after all, Goldney built his Aladdin's Cave primarily for himself, and whenever respectable Quakerdom became too stifling, he escaped underground into a romantic dream world. Who knows?

Many unanswered questions linger around Goldney Grotto, but it is an open book compared with the grotto at Warmley. This strange suite of caverns is undoubtedly eighteenth-century, but there is no record of when or how it was

*The central chamber at Warmley Grotto*

The entrance to the grotto is in a public park which used to be the grounds of Warmley House. The House is now a private retirement home, but the grounds remain a fascinating landmark of the industrial revolution. The Warmley estate was established in 1746 by William Champion, who invented and patented a revolutionary new zinc-making process and pioneered integrated brass manufacture. In Warmley, he built what was probably the first self-contained industrial complex, including not only brass, copper and zinc works, but cottages for his workers and a mansion for himself.

Champion was an eccentric genius whose life story reads like a Greek tragedy. In his youth, he is said to have dressed as a pauper and travelled Europe for six years, discovering the secrets of brass and zinc manufacture. Back home, he became an industrial king, ruling over Europe's largest and most successful brass foundry. But the breadth of vision which made his fortune destroyed him in the end. His inventive mind seethed with grand schemes. In 1767, for example, he proposed creating a floating harbour in the centre of Bristol; but he was way ahead of his time, and it was another 40 years before this excellent idea was pursued. Eventually, Champion over-reached himself. The failure of an ambitious docks project and over-diversification stretched his finances to the limit. In 1769, his company collapsed and the Warmley works were sold to his arch-rival, Harford's and Bristol Brass and Copper Company. The new owners did very well out of

built, what visitors thought of it, or what they did there. The first written evidence of the grotto is a church magazine dated 1908, which briefly mentions it as one of the attractions at a summer fête. For two centuries, Warmley Grotto seems to have been ignored, neglected, even used as a pig-sty. It is only in recent years that dedicated local historians have uncovered its secrets.

***Above and below: parts of the Warmley Grotto labyrinth***

Champion's inventions, and legend has it that, some years later, they sought out the ruined genius to offer him an annuity. They found him working as a mason in Liverpool but, as befits a tragic hero, he declined their offer.

Like Thomas Goldney III, Champion was a Quaker, and he was related to Goldney by marriage. He must have known the Clifton garden and grotto, and no doubt took some inspiration from them, but the landscape he created at Warmley is very different. Champion's gardens are like their creator—larger than life and workaholic. Everything is on an enormous scale, and even ornamental features are closely connected with industry. The focal point of the grounds used to be a 13-acre lake, which also served as a reservoir to feed the water mills at the foundries. It is now dry, but the immense statue of Neptune that once loomed out of the middle of it still stands. Four times taller than an average man, he is a crude yet powerful figure— partly made of smooth plaster and partly of rough black clinker waste from the works.

*Champion's Neptune: a giant, like his creator*

a redundant foundry. He also recycled the spiky waste from the zinc process to give a rough, cave-like texture to the walls. There are no shells, crystals, statues or pretty decorations. All is dark and melancholy. The only light seeps through small roof openings, except in the central chamber, which has been open to the sky since the roof caved in, probably long ago.

It is all very strange. Is the grotto simply unfinished? Maybe Champion intended to decorate it in the course of time—although one cannot imagine him fiddling about with shells and knick-knacks. The grand gesture was more his style, and the grotto may have relied on spectacular use of water, light and even pyrotechnics. Excavation has uncovered a superb hydraulic system and some tantalising evidence which may point to other "special effects". In one chamber, for example, there was a 20-foot/6-metre waterfall which cascaded down from a hidden water-tank. On the left is a culvert leading up to the tank which appears to

Sheer size is the most impressive feature of the grotto, too. Built inside an artificial mound, it is a rambling network of great vaulted tunnels and chambers—some with a ceiling height of over 23 feet/7 metres—which house a complex system of cascades, water channels and pools. Two of these pools seem too deep to have been made for ornamental purposes. It is likely that they were originally industrial tanks, and that practical Champion built his grotto over have no purpose. It is possible that this was used to create a pall of smoke or steam—just the sort of trick to appeal to the ingenious Champion.

All this is speculation—as is so much else about Warmley Grotto. Its many baffling features inspire numerous theories. One of the wildest is a suggestion that it is not a folly at all, but an eccentrically-

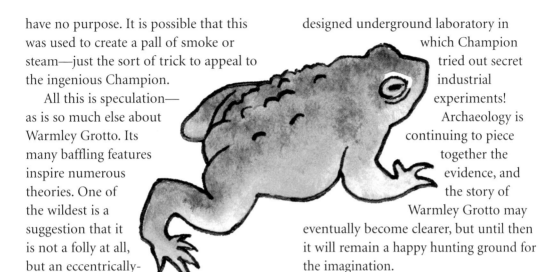

designed underground laboratory in which Champion tried out secret industrial experiments! Archaeology is continuing to piece together the evidence, and the story of Warmley Grotto may eventually become clearer, but until then it will remain a happy hunting ground for the imagination.

## access information grottoes

### Goldney Grotto:

Goldney Hall, which is now a University Hall of Residence, holds occasional Open Days in spring and summer, when you can see the grounds and grotto. You will find details on their website: www.goldneyhall.com

Or ring 0117 903 4880.

It is also possible to hire the orangery and grounds (including access to the grotto) for weddings, functions, tours and events.

For details, ring the Goldney Business Office on 0117 903 4873.

### Warmley Grotto:

You can enjoy a guided walk around Champion's Warmley estate and grotto at these times:

All year round: 2nd Sunday of each month, start 2pm.

In addition, from March to October: 4th Sunday of each month, start 2pm.

Also spring and summer bank holidays.

Meet at the Windmill Tower, Tower Lane, Warmley.

The Windmill Tower also houses Kingswood Museum, run by volunteers and open on the same afternoons as the walks, as well as each Tuesday 2-5pm.

If you need more information, ring 0117 9564896 or 0117 967 5711

# Caves

# From Knicker Nitch

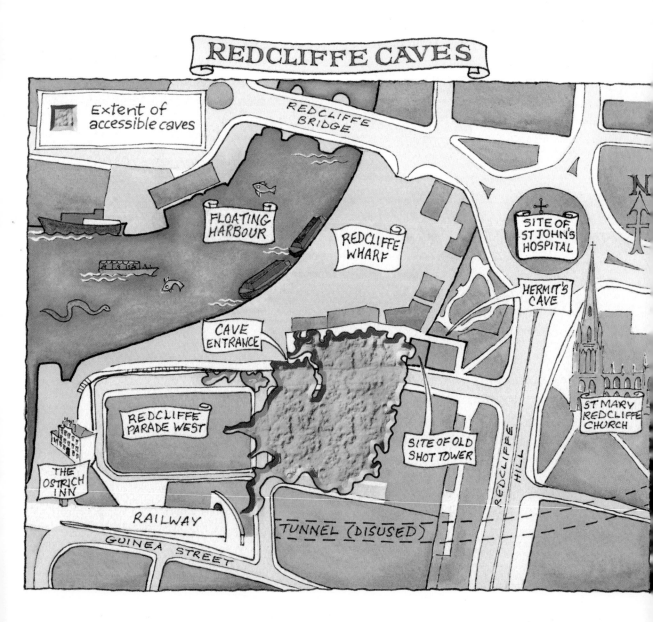

REDCLIFFE CAVES

Extent of accessible caves

REDCLIFFE BRIDGE

FLOATING HARBOUR

REDCLIFFE WHARF

SITE OF ST JOHN'S HOSPITAL

HERMIT'S CAVE

CAVE ENTRANCE

REDCLIFFE PARADE WEST

ST MARY REDCLIFFE CHURCH

SITE OF OLD SHOT TOWER

REDCLIFFE HILL

THE OSTRICH INN

RAILWAY

GUINEA STREET

TUNNEL (DISUSED)

# to Smuggler's Bottom

Caves are one of Bristol's best-kept underground secrets. From the vast vault of Pen Park Hole to the eerie caverns beneath Redcliffe, the region is pitted with them. Many have never been fully explored and most are seldom visited. Nevertheless, every Bristolian has a cave story to tell. Smugglers, slaves, hermits . . . legends swirl like mist around Bristol's caves.

None has inspired more tales than Redcliffe Caves—and no wonder. Exploring this underground labyrinth is enough to fire even the most sluggish imagination. It is like being lost in a petrified forest. Everywhere, there are great stone "tree trunks" arching over chambers and passages which lead off into the darkness. Here and there, incongruous walls and shafts seem to have taken root. Everything is deep red and the silence is complete.

No-one knows how large Redcliffe Caves are. Behind a small, locked entrance in the cliffs on Redcliffe Wharf, accessible caves fan out for well over an acre beneath the streets of Redcliffe. Beyond these, walls and infill block the way, but there are certainly more caverns. Contractors digging deep foundations or tunnels for cables and pipes have often discovered further parts of the labyrinth, some as much as half a mile away from Redcliffe Wharf.

For the most part, Redcliffe Caves were not formed by nature. The marks of tools make it clear that they have been quarried out of the soft red sandstone from which Redcliffe takes its name. The "tree trunks" are in fact pillars of stone left standing to hold up the roughly vaulted roof.

There may well have been small natural caves in the cliffs, carved out by the Avon's high tides, from the earliest times, and it is not clear when human excavation first started. Legend goes back as far as King Alfred, who is said to have hidden from marauding Danes in Redcliffe Caves, and the wharf in front of them used to be known as Alfred's Quay.

The story is probably a myth, but some excavation of the

21

Caves may have taken place in medieval times. By the twelfth century, Redcliffe had become a prosperous borough and an ecclesiastical building boom was under way, including the famous Church of St. Mary Redcliffe and the long-gone Hospital of St. John. Folklore tells that the monks of St. John's carved underground passages and cells for contemplation, and it was long believed that you could get down into Redcliffe Caves through a hollow pillar inside St. Mary's. Stories as old and tenacious as these often have some basis in fact. So perhaps medieval clerics did carve out some of Redcliffe Caves—although heaven knows for what purpose.

Only one tiny off-shoot of Redcliffe Caves—St. John's Hermitage—actually appears in medieval records. This is a small cave behind a locked, arched doorway which can still be seen in the park opposite St. Mary Redcliffe known as the Friends' Burial Ground. Here, a hermit called John Sparkes was "placed" by Thomas Lord Berkeley in 1346 to pray for him and his family. It sounds a tedious life, but it obviously suited hermits down to the ground. A succession of them lived in the "little Tenement in the Rocke or Cliffe" until the seventeenth century. Inside the cave there is a gravestone dedicated to the last inhabitant, "Christopher the Monk or Christopher Birckhead", who died in 1669.

The bulk of Redcliffe Caves, however, almost certainly owe their existence to the less romantic needs of industry. Most were probably excavated for their fine sand, which is excellent for glass manufacture. Bristol developed a flourishing bottle-making industry from the seventeenth century, because the medicinal water from the City's famous Hot Well was exported all over the world (see next chapter). By 1724, there were 15 glass factories in Bristol, many of them in the Redcliffe area. The sandstone cliffs were the obvious place to find the necessary sand, but as Redcliffe was already built-up, it had to be mined from below, rather than quarried from the surface.

Abraham Lloyd, who owned Redcliffe Wharf for 50 years from 1726, no doubt excavated a good deal to supply his own

glass and pot factory. French and Spanish prisoners of war probably provided him with cheap labour for this task in the 1740s. It is unlikely that these unfortunates were incarcerated in the Caves, but there is a persistent story that, in some part of the labyrinth now lost, a cavern was once discovered which had stone seats carved around the edges and shackles on the floor. This may have given rise to one of Bristol's most enduring myths: that hordes of slaves were kept in Redcliffe Caves to await deportation.

This is almost certainly bunkum. It is true that many of Bristol's most prominent merchants made their fortunes from the shameful trade in African slaves, but most never laid eyes on their human "product". A few kept black personal servants, but they never brought shiploads of slaves to Bristol. The slaving ships sailed a triangular route. From Bristol they made for West Africa laden with gin, arms and trinkets which were exchanged for slaves. From there, they sailed to the American and West Indian colonies where the slaves were sold. They then returned home with cargoes of tobacco and molasses. If Redcliffe Caves are haunted, it isn't by ghostly slaves.

Smugglers are more likely candidates. It seems that, towards the end of the eighteenth century, excavation of the Caves was coming to an end, and they were being used as warehouses. Only the more accessible areas would have been used, and it appears that the true extent of the catacombs was gradually forgotten. The deeper caverns, abandoned by legitimate business, would have made ideal hiding-places for contraband.

More and more of the Caves were "lost" as time went on. Some were blocked off by walls built to separate storage spaces, and others were filled with piles of waste. The Caves were used as a rubbish dump not only by glass and pottery factories but also by William Watts' famous Shot Tower. Watts was a plumber who invented a method of making molten lead into perfectly rounded shot by dropping it from a great height into water. In the 1780s, he converted his home on Redcliffe Hill into a factory by deepening the well in the basement and building a tower on top. This Shot Tower continued in successful production until 1968 when, sadly, it was demolished for road-widening.

There is a story that Watts was inspired by a dream in which his wife stood on top of St. Mary Redcliffe and dropped molten lead on him through the holes of a frying pan. Be that as it may, Watts patented his process with such success that Bristol poet John Dix was moved to pen these immortal lines:

*Mr. Watts very soon a patent got*
*So that very soon only himself*
*could make Patent Shot;*
*And King George and his son*
*declar'd that they'd not*
*Shoot with anything else—*
*and they ordered a lot.*

Watts dumped the toxic ash from his furnaces into Redcliffe Caves. This, combined with all the other masonry and debris, made large sections of the Caves inaccessible and they were forgotten. In 1868, when a tunnel for the Harbour Railway was being excavated near Guinea

Street, workmen were amazed to find part of the labyrinth. Caverns apparently extended well beyond the far side of the trench, but the tunnel has sealed these off ever since.

Only the Caves nearest the river continued to be used. In the nineteenth century they provided storage space for companies trading with Africa—which may be where the slave story comes from—and in this century for the LMS Railway. During the Blitz, some desperate citizens commandeered the Caves as a bomb shelter, but

*Redcliffe Caves being used for storage, c.1890*

they were not as safe as they appeared. Bombs that destroyed Redcliffe Infants' School also opened up a crater in the caverns below.

In the 1950s, when trade in the City Docks declined rapidly, the Caves were locked up and fell into complete disuse. They are rarely visited, although they have provided an atmospheric setting for several films and TV programmes such as *Robin Hood, Casualty* and *Relic Hunter*. However, if plans to "develop" Redcliffe Wharf ever come to fruition, Redcliffe Caves may again be open for business— this time as a tourist attraction.

This fate will certainly never befall Pen Park Hole—an immense natural cavern which yawns beneath a park at the junction of Pen Park Road and Charlton Road in North Bristol. It is an ancient, pre-Triassic formation, consisting of several shafts and passages leading to a huge underground chamber with a lake at the bottom. The roof of the chamber is only 20 feet/6 metres below ground level, but the floor drops to an incredible 183 feet/55 metres (nearly as deep as the Avon Gorge). From time to time, the level of the lake fluctuates by over 50 feet/15 metres— although why it should, and what its source is, have never been convincingly explained.

Pen Park Hole was probably first discovered by lead miners centuries ago. There is some evidence of mining, and a few remains of tobacco pipes and old shoes dating from around 1590 have been discovered. The Hole was already known to be old by the time one "Captain Sturmey, a warm, inquisitive seaman" explored it in 1669. One of his party was "affrighted by the sight of an evil spirit"—and who can blame him? A huge, underground chasm with a seemingly bottomless lake is the stuff of nightmares.

Nevertheless, the Hole excited considerable interest in the eighteenth century, particularly amongst clergymen. The Rev. A. Catcott, in his Treatise on the Deluge, cited the lake as proof that Noah's Flood had covered the whole world. He never ventured down himself, however, leaving the risky work of exploration to his brother. A fellow cleric, the Rev. Thomas Newman, was not so circumspect. While peering down one of the entrance shafts in 1775, he fell to his

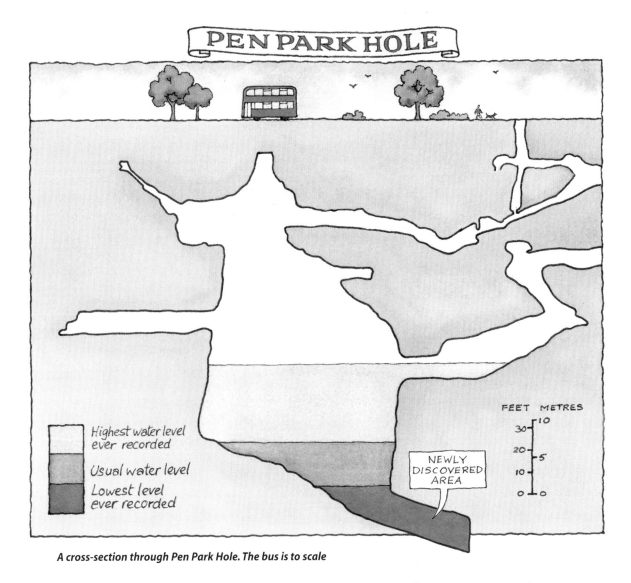

# PEN PARK HOLE

Highest water level ever recorded

Usual water level

Lowest level ever recorded

NEWLY DISCOVERED AREA

FEET   METRES

*A cross-section through Pen Park Hole. The bus is to scale*

death. It was six weeks before his body was recovered. Soon after this unfortunate incident, the three shafts that gave access to the cave from the surface were sealed off. Since then, the Hole has been opened only on rare occasions for experienced cavers. There is still much to explore. Recently, one brave caver dived into the claustrophobic depths of the lake and discovered a previously unknown underwater shaft that goes far deeper than the lake floor. There may yet be more to discover.

The Avon Gorge is more accessible territory for cavers, and the rocks are often festooned with their ropes. The limestone cliffs are dimpled with numerous small caves on both sides of the river. Exactly how many is difficult to say. Various surveys have been published, but none is completely reliable. Cavers themselves have added to the confusion,

*Descending into the depths of Pen Park Hole*
*Photo: Graham Mullan*

because they delight in bestowing original names on their "discoveries". One cave may therefore collect several names, and later be recorded as several different caves.

Fanciful names are often inspired by the strange articles which have found their way into the caves. Take Knicker Nitch (frilly underwear) and Porno's Pot (under-the-counter magazines), for example. Since both these caves are about 200 feet/60 metres above the river, and gaining access necessitates shinning up or down sheer rock, one cannot help wondering what strange compulsion drove the original owners to deposit these articles.

Some of the Avon Gorge caves have much older and more respectable tales to tell. On the Clifton side of the Avon, at Horseshoe Bend, is a large cave with a fascinating history. Its modern name is Boat Cave—because the remains of an old boat were found there—but it used to be known as the Holywell of Shirehampton, or Bucklewell ("the well of bowing down"). Inside, there is crumbling masonry—the remains of an ancient shrine or hermitage—and a pool fed by a stream which seeps through the floor of the cave. The rays of the midsummer sun are said to strike the centre of this pool, and seers used to read the future in its depths. The water was renowned as a cure for sore eyes, and hopeful visitors apparently threw offerings into the pool. The less devout no doubt retrieved these valuables later, which is probably why the rumour grew that there was hidden treasure buried in the Bucklewell.

Near the Suspension Bridge is one of the most interesting—and accessible—of all the caves. It is set into the cliff face 90 feet/27 metres below the edge of the

Downs, but can be approached via a 200-foot/60-metre tunnel from the Observatory. This tunnel was built in 1837 by William West, the Observatory's creator, presumably so that he could enjoy the cave's breathtaking view over the Gorge. The cavern is usually known as Giant's Cave, but it has numerous other names, including Ghyston's Cave, St. Vincent's Chapel and Fox Hole. The cave's history is equally confusing. It is supposed to be the site of an ancient chapel or hermitage, but whether this was

*Cavers scaling the Avon Gorge*

actually inside the cave or on a ledge outside is not clear. William Wyrecestre, an indefatigable fifteenth-century surveyor of Bristol buildings, made his way down the narrow ledge which used to

*Giant's Cave with the Suspension Bridge beyond*

**The view from Giant's Cave. Above: in 1837, painted by E. G. Müller; below: as it is today.**

lead to the cave and measured the hermitage. The dimensions of the building he records are too large to have fitted into the cave, so perhaps it jutted out onto a ledge which, like the path, has now eroded away. Or maybe Wyrecestre simply got the measurements wrong (he sometimes did). Some artefacts that were

found in the cave—including, apparently, Roman pottery, church tiles and a portion of Gothic window—might hold the key to its history. But they were lost during the First World War. The only certainty is that, if any holy men lived in the cave, they were gone by 1804, when "a gang of robbers who had long been the terror of Clifton" were captured there.

The full story of Giant's Cave will probably never be established, and the same applies to most of Bristol's caves. Legends abound, but facts seem impossible to pin down. The stories are always ambiguous, the evidence

tantalisingly inconclusive. Some caves are so elusive they actually disappear. Whatever happened to Smuggler's Bottom, for example? This reputed hiding-place for contraband is supposed to have been on the banks of the Frome at Stapleton. It's been recorded—even photographed—but nobody appears to know where it is any more.

The caves of Bristol seem determined to keep their secrets. But who would want it any other way? Mystery is part of their charm.

## access information caves

### Redcliffe Caves:

These are normally closed to the public. However, Alan Gray, who is a local caver and expert on Redcliffe Caves, occasionally guides parties around the more accessible areas.
Alan has a website: www.bristoltours.com
Or you can contact him by email on: toursandresearch@yahoo.com

### Giant's Cave:

This can be accessed via a tunnel running from the Observatory on the Downs, near the Suspension Bridge. The Observatory is only open "weather permitting" and at rather erratic times. You are most likely to find it open12.30-4pm on weekdays and 10.30-4pm at weekends.

# Hot livers, feeble brains

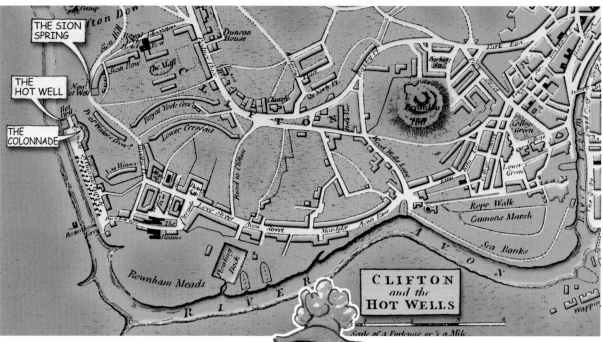

THE SION SPRING

THE HOT WELL

THE COLONNADE

CLIFTON and the HOT WELLS

*The Clifton and Hot Wells area c. 1794*

One of Bristol's most fascinating subterranean features is not merely underground, but underwater a good deal of the time. The hot spring that once made Bristol a world-famous spa discharges beneath the level of the Avon for all but one and a half hours a day at low tide. For this short period, it is possible to see it gurgling out of the river's muddy banks below Hotwell Road just south of the Suspension Bridge.

Insignificant as it may look, this is no ordinary spring. The water emerges hot (76°F/23°C) and effervescent. According to an analysis conducted in 1912, it is also 170 times more radioactive than the public water supply. Apparently, first-time drinkers of this brew experienced something akin to intoxication. This startling property was taken as a sure sign of medicinal powers, and for centuries Bristol's Hot Well was believed to cure everything from diabetes to consumption.

# and red pimply faces

Until well into the nineteenth century, people were inclined to clutch at straws when it came to their health. Medical science tended to be a hit or miss affair, heavily reliant on savage surgery, blood-letting and leeches. No wonder everyone longed for gentler and surer remedies.

Whether the waters of Bristol's Hot Well have any true medicinal benefits has never been proved one way or the other. But to bathe and take the waters in the spectacularly beautiful setting of the Avon

*The "sublime scenery" around the Hot Well spa complex in the 1790s. Painting by J. M. W. Turner*

HARROGATE v. HOTWELLS
Mr. J. H. Howell, J.P.,—"Very sorry, my lord, that your health necessitates your leaving us for a time: in the meanwhile can we send you a few bottles of our own brew?"

*There was always fierce rivalry between Britain's Spas*

Luckily, the less athletic could also benefit from the waters in bottled form. Unlike Bath Spa water, it kept well, and by the end of the seventeenth century it was being sent all over the world. Bristol's flourishing glass-making industry was based on the huge demand for bottles which this trade created.

The increasing fame of the Hot Well attracted the attention of the Society of Merchant Venturers, and

Gorge must have been a pleasant experience. Rest, fresh air and optimism may indeed have worked wonders.

The Hot Well's history goes back at least as far as the fifteenth century, when scurvy-ridden sailors appear to have pinned their faith on it. By 1630, the spring's reputation had grown to such an extent that an entrepreneur obtained a licence to "take in" the Hot Well water and make baths for visitors.

The enterprise obviously took off quickly. By 1634, three Cavaliers from Norwich reported "a good store of company" at the Hot Well. Visitors washed in the well and drank the water after descending the "rocky and steep-winding and craggy way neere 200 slippery steps" which led to the spring. In view of the intoxicating effects of the water, the journey back must have been fraught with hazard. Even the doughty Cavaliers admit to having "laid aside our commanding postures".

*The earliest known illustration of the Hot Well from Millerd's map of 1673, showing [some of] the "neere 200 slippery steps"*

*Georgian High Society flocked to Bristol's Hot Well*

in 1676 they purchased it along with the Manor of Clifton. For some years after, the fortunes of the spring were mixed. As its outlet is usually below the level of the Avon, keeping the spring water uncontaminated by the sewage-laden river was a continual battle, and several attempts were made to solve the problem with indifferent success.

On the other hand, the reputation of the spring as a cure grew apace. In 1677, Queen Catherine of Braganza, the unfortunate wife of Charles II, bestowed royal patronage by sampling the waters. Three years later, the spring received an even greater boost in the humble shape of John Gagg, a diabetic baker of Castle Street. One night he dreamt that he must drink the Hot Well water, and he wasted no time in turning the dream into reality.

According to Mr. Gagg, he was cured within days. This case became so famous that the Hot Well grew to be regarded as an infallible cure for diabetes.

The water was believed to be excellent physick against numerous other conditions. The first medical book on the Hot Well, published in 1703, gives a formidable list, including "hot livers, feeble brains and red pimply faces", not to mention "slipperiness of parts".

In 1695, the Merchant Venturers granted a 90-year lease on the Hot Well to Charles Jones, a soap boiler, and Thomas Callow Hill, a draper, for an annual rent of £5, on condition that they spend £500 on developing the area. Facilities included a pump room, lodging houses and walks giving better access to the well. To protect the spring from contamination, Jones and Hill invested in an elaborate system of pumps and valves which raised the outlet above high water mark.

The new pump room became the scene of many a glittering society function. When a handsome assembly room was added to the facilities in 1723, the Hot Well attracted more and more fashionable pleasure-lovers as well as invalids. High Society flocked—including the Duchess of Marlborough, the Duchess of Kent, Lady Diana Spencer and Lord Romney. They disported themselves at lavish breakfasts, evening balls, and outdoor entertainments such as ferry trips to Long Ashton for strawberries and cream, tandem rides on "double horses" and river cruises with musical accompaniment.

The resort's success meant more lodging-houses were needed and building began in Dowry Square in the 1720s. Many fashionable medical men set up in practice here and it became a local Harley Street.

Theatre was all the rage, and in 1729 a playhouse was built at Jacob's Wells. It was conveniently sited next to The Malt and Shovel ale house, and a hole was made in the party wall so that refreshment could be passed through to spectators and actors.

Meanwhile, a more austere type of visitor was being attracted to a rival hot spring situated on the Avon Gorge a little further from the City. This spring, known as the New Hot Well (later St. Vincent's

*Above: John Wesley, portrait by J. Harley, 1745*
*Below: The Colonnade—almost the only part of the Georgian Hot Well complex that still survives*

*The last vestiges of St. Vincent's Spring*

white egg and that old, unfashionable medicine, Prayer".

St. Vincent's Spring enjoyed a brief vogue, but it could never compete with the Hot Well. Access was dangerous for invalids, and the lonely location was hardly conducive to pleasure-seeking. One dejected visitor wrote: "The nearest dwelling is a mile distant and the only human objects ordinarily visible are the gibbeted remains of two murderers."

By the end of the eighteenth century St. Vincent's Spring had had its day. Later, attempts were made to tap its waters for the supply of Clifton and the surrounding areas, and in 1894, a public drinking fountain was installed. This was still operational into the 1960s, but by 1975 the pipework had been vandalised and

Spring), produced a similar water, although slightly cooler and less radioactive. It was first developed around 1730, when a pump room and lodging house were built. As the only access to the spring was via a rocky horse track from Durdham Down, it only attracted visitors of stoic character and sound limb. The most famous of these was John Wesley, the founder of Methodism, who came to drink the waters in 1754. The proprietors trumpeted his recovery from what they claimed was "a greedy consumption (which) had determined to put an end to his days". Wesley himself attributed his cure to a combination of the waters with a "plaster of brimstone with

*Ann Yearsley, one of the Hot Well's more flamboyant personalities*

*The Royal Clifton Spa, James Bolton's attempt to revive the Hot Well's fortunes in the 1820s*

the tap was out of commission. Today, the only surface evidence of St. Vincent's Spring is a spout set into a stone on the cliff face next to the Portway near Black Rocks Quarry.

While St. Vincent's Spring faded out in the latter half of the eighteenth century, the original Hot Well enjoyed the heyday of its popularity. Trade was so brisk that a second Assembly Room was built, and in 1785 the Colonnade—a kind of shopping mall—completed the facilities. Part of this building can still be seen beside Hotwell Road.

The Hot Well's incomparable setting in the rugged grandeur of the Avon Gorge was the secret of its success. Being inexpensive into the bargain, the spa embodied the eighteenth century ideal of "elegant economy".

The Hot Well was a summer resort, unlike Bath, so there was no direct competition. Many tradesmen and clients moved from one to the other as the seasons turned, and the two spas complemented each other very nicely. Bath was rather formal and aristocratic, while the Hot Well had a free and easy—not to say risqué—charm.

Dr. Andrew Carrick wrote of the scene in 1786: "It was then during the Summer one of the best frequented and most crowded water places in the Kingdom. Scores of the nobility were to be found there every season . . . Three extensive taverns were constantly full and two spacious ballrooms were profitably kept open. There was a well attended ball, a public breakfast and a promenade every week, and often twice a week. The pump room was all day long the resort of invalids . . . The adjoining walk was filled with fashionable company; the sublime scenery of the cliffs was enlivened by the sounds of music; the downs and the avenues to The Hot Well were filled with strings of carriages and with parties on horseback and on foot."

The Hot Well became so famous that it was immortalised in literature. Fanny Burney made it the setting for her vivacious novel *Evelina* and William Whitehead—a Poet Laureate of towering insignificance—published a lengthy extravaganza entitled *Hymn to the Nymph of the Bristol Spring*. For a while, the spring even boasted a real literary nymph in Anne Yearsley—a milkmaid turned poetess who operated a circulating library from the Colonnade.

In 1793, a Clifton attorney who lived on Sion Hill attempted to set up a rival spa. He blasted a 246-foot shaft down through St. Vincent's Rock and tapped a hot spring—presumably from the same source as the Hot Well. He built a pump room (reputedly on the site of Sion House), but the venture soon failed.

The Sion Spring enterprise was extremely ill-timed, as the Hot Well itself was in deep trouble by the 1790s. Tidal contamination was again a problem, and to offset the cost of remedial work,

*Taking the waters at the Royal Clifton Spa*

Samuel Powell—who took over the lease in 1790—increased charges by about 260%. Worse still, Dr. Thomas Beddoes of Dowry Square cast doubt upon the water's ability to cure consumption. He believed cows' breath was a more effective cure, and took cattle into his patients' bedrooms to prove it. Dr. Beddoes' assistant, Humphry Davy, experimented with nitrous oxide (laughing gas), so if clients fancied a change from cows' breath, they could inhale a lungful from Davy's green bag and run giggling round the Square.

Despite these eccentric activities, Dr. Beddoes' views carried weight, and his contempt for the Hot Well's curative powers sounded the death knell for the spa. Within a few seasons, the flood of visitors dwindled to a trickle. Only the

*Above: Remains of the very last phase of the Hot Well—George Newnes'*
*late Victorian pump room beside the Avon Gorge Hotel. Inset: detail from*
*the pediment above the entrance to Newnes' Bath House*
*Below: Dowry Square showing Dr. Beddoes' Pneumatic Institute in the foreground with Humphry Davy's*
*wysteria-covered house in the far corner of the square*

desperate now came—mainly incurable consumptives nursing one last hope. A group of lodging-houses near the spring became known as Death Row.

In 1822, Mr. James Bolton made a plucky attempt to revive the spa. The old Hot Well Pump Room was demolished and a handsome new building called The Royal Clifton Spa was erected. Mineral baths and spa water were provided, of course, but health was not the only thing on sale. Bolton hedged his bets by offering numerous other commodities, including portable seats, fossils, knife-cleaning machines, Hot Well tooth powder and boomerangs. It was a brave try, but after a short period of limited revival, the Hot Well again fell from popularity. In 1867, the Royal Clifton Spa was demolished, along with the craggy rock called Hot Well Point, to allow for widening of the river. However, the spring was preserved and the water was drawn up to a pump in a stone arch. This arch can still be seen beside Hotwell Road, although spa water is no longer pumped to it.

*The arch over the fountain beside Hotwell Road. The spa water was pumped here for general public use from 1877 until 1913, when it became so polluted that it was declared unfit for consumption*

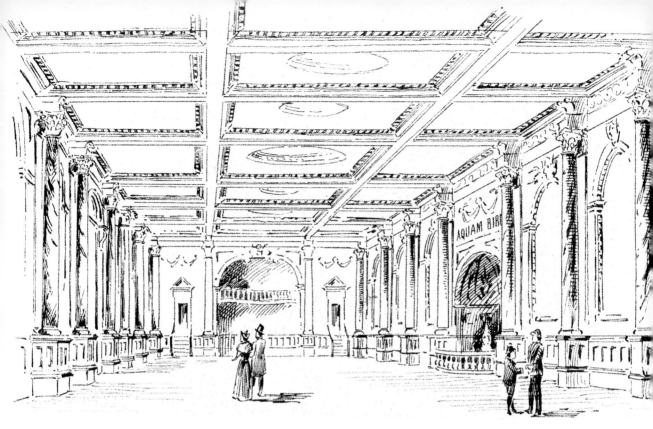

*George Newnes' Hydropathic Institute in the 1890s*

As the nineteenth century drew to a close, the spa seemed dead and buried. The Hotwells area, clustered around the increasingly sewage-encrusted banks of the Avon, became smelly and disreputable. Health was the last thing anyone would seek there.

Nevertheless, the enterprising Merchant Venturers, who still owned the site, were not defeated. In the 1890s, they tried once more to resurrect the spa—not in Hotwells itself this time, but on top of St. Vincent's Rock in healthy, fashionable Clifton. It would mean pumping the spring water all the way up through the Rock, but the very man to do it had presented himself: George Newnes—MP, publisher and energetic entrepreneur. When he applied to the Venturers to build the Clifton Rocks Railway from Hotwells to Clifton (see next chapter), they seized their opportunity. They consented to the

Railway, but only on condition that Newnes also construct a "Hydropathic Institute" next to the upper station in Clifton.

Newnes did nothing by halves, and although the Hydropathic Institute was thrust upon him, he made an excellent job of it. In 1894, he opened a spectacular Grand Pump Room, and four years later the Grand Spa Hotel (now the Avon Gorge Hotel) was built next to it. The grandiose Pump Room, with its lavish "Corinthian style" marbles and superb view of the Gorge, was advertised as "a building second to none in point of grandeur and completeness for its purpose of any health resort in the World". Nevertheless, the new spa never quite lived up to its promise. The Avon Gorge had been exotic enough for

Georgian visitors, but well-travelled Edwardians found it rather tame compared with the Continental glamour of Baden Baden or Aix.

The Grand Pump Room's marble fountain dispensed its healing waters for barely 20 years. By 1920, the building had been turned into a cinema, and in the 1950s and 60s it was used as a dance hall. Now, it seems to have become an embarrassment, and is languishing, unused and neglected, beside the Avon Gorge Hotel. The ruined interior is a surreal jumble. Geometric plastic chandeliers hang from ornate moulded ceilings, and huge Victorian marble maidens languish beside hideous vinyl counters from the brothel-creeper era.

This abandoned building, together with the Colonnade and the fountain arch beside Hotwell Road, are all that remains from the Hot Well's long and colourful history. It seems incredibly little, but the spa's success never depended on bricks and mortar. The Avon Gorge provided a far more beautiful setting than any building. The Gorge is still there— and the spring itself still bubbles up from its mysterious underground source. So who knows? Perhaps the Hot Well is not finished yet. One day we may again take its famous waters.

*Echoes of past splendour: the abandoned pump room of the Hydropathic Institute as it is today*

# Penny up,

Travelling north along Hotwell Road towards the Portway, just before passing under the Suspension Bridge, you have probably noticed what appears to be the façade of a house built into the cliff face. Look closely at this crumbling edifice, and you will be able to make out the puzzling legend "CLIFON ROKS RILWAY" carved on the battered lintel. This is the entrance to a forgotten engineering masterpiece: The Clifton Rocks Railway.

Funicular railways are common enough—but most are built in the open air. The Clifton Rocks Railway was—with the greatest difficulty—constructed inside the cliffs of the Avon Gorge. Behind the lower station on Hotwell Road, a 500-foot/150-metre tunnel rises at a sharp 1:2.2 gradient to emerge on the top of St. Vincent's Rock, beside the Avon Gorge Hotel. The upper station is a derelict, triangular building on the corner of Sion Hill and Princes Lane. It is ignominiously shrouded in hardboard nowadays, but if you peer through the cracks, you can still see remnants of its former glory. The staircases, surrounded by handsome wrought-ironwork, still lead down to the

*The lower station as it is today*

# Ha'penny down

CLIFTON ROCKS RAILWAY

*A cut-away illustration showing the course of the railway through the cliff*

platform. Over this, there are the remains of a pavement made of small glass panels. This was a kind of viewing platform, through which sightseers could marvel at the railway in action.

Many Cliftonians would like to see their unique railway restored, but when it was built they didn't really want it. In the late nineteenth century, Clifton was a genteel residential area. Hotwells, on the

*Above: the lower station in Hotwells, c. 1900*
*Below: the upper station in Clifton, c. 1912*

other hand, had gone very down-market since the demise of the spa. It was now a dingy, disreputable place with a shifting population of assorted seafarers. The Avon was a stinking open sewer, and the inhabitants of its banks appeared equally unsavoury to the snobbish residents of Clifton. The last thing they wanted was a railway to ferry hordes of drunken sailors up to their fashionable domain. In fact, they favoured complete isolation from workaday Bristol, and even resisted the introduction of trams into their elegant streets.

Eventually, of course, connection with Bristol's developing public transport system became inevitable. In 1880 a proposal was put forward to build an inclined railway down the face of the Avon Gorge. This would connect Clifton with both the City Tramway at Hotwells and the terminus of the Port and Pier Railway, which ran from Hotwells to Avonmouth. The Merchant Venturers, who owned the cliffs, rejected the idea because it would be such an eyesore.

*photo courtesy Peter Davey Collection*

In 1890, the entrepreneur George Newnes came up with an answer which would leave the scenic beauty of the Gorge unmarred: a funicular railway running through the rock in a tunnel. The Merchant Venturers consented—on condition that Newnes also try to resurrect Bristol as a spa town by pumping the Hot Well water up to Clifton and constructing a "Hydropathic Institute" next to the railway's upper station (see previous chapter).

It was an irritating condition, but Newnes was not deterred. He was a man of many enthusiasms, and had a particular passion for funicular railways. He had already collaborated with the eminent engineer G. Croydon Marks on the famous Lynton/Lynmouth Cliff Railway in Devon, and both men found conquering the Avon Gorge an irresistible challenge. Newnes put up the money, Bristol architect Philip Munroe joined the team, and together they planned a *tour de force* of funicular engineering.

Excavation got under way in March 1891. It was a daunting and dangerous task. At the time, the tunnel was the widest of its kind in the world, and the limestone through which it was cut was crazed with faults. In parts it was so conglomerated with other rocks that it broke the drills. In others it was so loose that tunnelling caused huge rock falls—both inside and out. One such, which occurred just six weeks before the opening of the railway, hurtled down the cliff face and narrowly missed a passing

**Building the railway, 1891**

photo courtesy Peter Davey Collection

*The famous railway featured on many hand-tinted postcards*

them. There was still a good deal to be done, however, and after numerous delays and crises the construction eventually took two years instead of the scheduled 12 months, and cost Newnes £30,000—three times the original estimate.

Nevertheless, no corners were cut and the finished railway represented state-of-the-art technology. The tunnel was reinforced with a thick brick lining and was lit by gas lamps. Inside, four cars, connected in pairs by steel cables, were drawn up and down rails by the "water balance" technique. Each car had a tank built into the frame and, at the beginning of each journey, the top car was weighted with water so that it was heavy enough to draw up the bottom one as it descended. To get the balance right, the operator of the lower car used an electric telegraph to inform his opposite number in the upper car how many passengers he was carrying. The correct amount of water could then be added to the upper car's tank. When it reached the bottom, the water was automatically pumped back to a reservoir at the top.

Safety standards were "such as to satisfy the requirements of the most nervous of passengers". Each pair of cars had no fewer than three sets of duplicate brakes. One was operated by a "dead man's handle", another regulated speed and the third was an automatic system which would be activated in the extremely unlikely event of cable failure.

horse-tram. This sort of thing made the workforce jittery, and it was difficult to keep men for more than a few weeks.

The tunnel was dug from both ends at the same time, and the builders were haunted by the awful possibility that a tiny miscalculation might mean the two shafts didn't line up properly. Jubilation broke out when they did at last meet in the middle, and the contractor's 10-year-old son squeezed through the first hole knocked between

The Clifton Rocks Railway. 291.

*The railway in action*

the return journey. Instead of a ticket, they received a gilded metal medallion as a souvenir of the great occasion. Trade continued to be brisk for the first year, with around 11,000 passengers a week paying a penny to go up, and a ha'penny to go down.

Unfortunately, the railway never again reached such heights of popularity. To travel on it once was an experience not to be missed, but few people had cause to use it regularly. To go from the City Centre to Clifton via Hotwells is not, after all, the most logical route, and as buses, trams and cars made in-roads even into isolationist Clifton, the Rocks Railway became a curiosity rather than a practical means of getting about.

The Clifton Rocks Railway caused a sensation when it opened on 11 March 1893. On the first day, 6,220 people made

*An ice cream vendor outside the lower station, 1890s*

PURE I

*photo courtesy Peter Davey Collection*

Passenger numbers declined steadily. The worst blow came in 1922, when Hotwell Road was widened. This entailed the demolition of the Port and Pier Railway between Hotwells and Sneyd Park, which had been a useful connection for the Rocks Railway. It also brought a major road within inches of the lower station, making access difficult. In 1934, after continued deficits, the four cars were lowered to the bottom for the last time and the Clifton Rocks Railway closed.

This was by no means the end of the story, however. During the Second World War, when bomb-proof

**The Port and Pier Railway tunnel**

premises of any sort were like gold-dust in Bristol, the tunnel was again called into active service. British Overseas Airways took over part of the upper section, as did a number of blitzed citizens. It was a damp, smelly shelter, in which people had to perch precariously on concrete ledges.

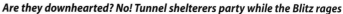

**Are they downhearted? No! Tunnel shelterers party while the Blitz rages**

50

Broadcasting House in London might be destroyed by bombs or even taken over by invading Nazis, it had decided to set up an emergency headquarters in Bristol.

The BBC's first choice had been the disused tunnel of the old Port and Pier Railway which runs under Bridge Valley Road. It was an ideal site and the BBC would have been well-advised to snap it up, but the Director-General saw no need for unseemly haste. Incredibly, he decided to send down a 100-strong symphony orchestra under

*Above: the lower station in 1941 converted into a BBC fortress, complete with anti-gas ventilation system*
*Above right: recording studio door still in place today*
*Below right: removal of the railway carriages to make way for the BBC*

Nevertheless, the old tunnel, with its memories of happier days, had a cheering effect. The sounds of concerts, sing-songs and fancy-dress parties drowned out the Luftwaffe.

Meanwhile, the BBC had its eye on the bottom section of the tunnel. Faced with the possibility that

51

the baton of Sir Adrian Boult to test the tunnel's acoustics before moving in. The maestro reported favourably, but the delay had proved fatal to the BBC's plans.

Bombing had now started in earnest and, because Bristol was terribly short of safe shelters, local people had taken refuge in the Port and Pier tunnel. It was

*Right: Old BBC machinery is still rusting in the tunnel*
*Below: The triangular site in the centre of this picture is all that remains of the upper station, now shrouded in hardboard*

wet, dark, insanitary and, as one investigator remarked, "deserved full marks for having everything that a shelter should not possess". Nevertheless, people had faith in its ability to protect them—unlike the official surface shelters. They had good reason to distrust these, as some had fallen down even before bombing started. So night after night, up to 3,000 people fought for a place in the tunnel. Despite opposition from Bristol Corporation, the shelterers became fond of their nightly home, and there was no winkling them out. On New Year's Day 1941, the BBC lined up wagons of equipment on the Portway ready to move in, but they were thwarted by a sit-in of 800 occupants. It was a clear victory for the people, and the BBC retreated gracefully.

The old Rocks Railway tunnel, despite the obvious drawback of being nearly vertical, was now the only option for the

*The lower station with the Suspension Bridge in the distance*

53

*Part of the tunnel as it is now*

BBC. In February 1941 the four carriages were removed and construction began in the lower station and the bottom part of the tunnel. Four large chambers were built, one above the other, housing a transmitter room, recording room, control room and studio which could take around a dozen actors and was equipped for music, drama and feature programmes. Emergency supplies included hundreds of hours of canned programmes and enough food and water to withstand a siege of several weeks. The old windows of the station were blocked up, and a special ventilation plant, designed to withstand gas attacks, was installed.

The control room was manned night and day throughout the War, transferring countless thousands of programmes to various transmitters. Thankfully, the main studios at BBC Bristol were never silenced, and the emergency studio never had to be used. But just in case, whenever the bombs began to fall on Bristol, key programme staff piled into an armoured Dodge shooting-brake and made a dash for the tunnel.

After the War, the transmitter continued to be used as a local booster station until 1960, when it became redundant and the BBC withdrew. A few years earlier, some nasty cracks had been noticed in the lower station's façade and the tunnel behind, and the steel and concrete buttresses which now disfigure the station had been constructed to shore it up.

The Clifton Rocks Railway has now mouldered quietly for over 40 years. The old stations are in a sorry state and the tunnel is filled with a jumble of relics from from the tunnel's service as a BOAC store, a bomb shelter and a BBC station. Concrete staircases run up each side, and between them are a series of strange rooms—some of which resemble steep, narrow cinemas, while others are full of antiquated radio equipment. It is estimated that 27,000 cubic feet/800 cubic metres of excess brick and concrete are now resident inside the tunnel.

*The desolate remains of the upper station*

Nevertheless, the old Rocks Railway continues to fascinate and new ideas for putting it to good use are frequently put forward. Unfortunately, the cost of conversion usually far outweighs the possible returns. It seems that the Clifton Rocks Railway is destined to remain what it has always been: an eccentric, exciting white elephant.

# Protect

If you travel from Bristol to London by train, you will enter a two-mile tunnel just east of Bath, between Box and Corsham. On both sides of this tunnel, unseen beneath the peaceful Wiltshire countryside, stretch acre after acre of

**Box Tunnel, western entrance**

huge fortified tunnels and chambers. This underground citadel was at the heart of Britain's desperate battle for survival in World War II.

Here, millions of tons of armaments were hidden from enemy bombers and vital aircraft production was protected in vast underground factories. Here, RAF Fighter Command controlled the battle of the skies from a subterranean control room. Even the Crown Jewels were brought here for safe keeping. By 1943, the whole complex had grown to 125 acres, and had cost well over four million pounds to construct.

The story of this wartime stronghold began in the mid-1930s, when politicians and military leaders watched developments in Hitler's Germany with growing unease. War seemed more and more inevitable and it was widely believed that air power would be the deciding factor. Building up stocks of armaments and protecting them from aerial bombing became a priority, and the search was on for underground sites.

Around Corsham, there were several extensive stone mines, some of which were still being worked,

# and survive

although the stone industry was in decline. These mines (confusingly known as quarries, although they are almost entirely underground) were deep enough to withstand the heaviest bombing, being 100 feet/30 metres below ground level. One of the largest of them, Tunnel Quarry, which lies to the north of Box Tunnel, offered another invaluable facility. It had a branch rail line which ran from deep inside the quarry to emerge at the eastern end of Box Tunnel and join the main GWR line a mile further east.

Tunnel Quarry was clearly the ideal site for an underground armaments depot. The War Office acquired it from the Bath & Portland Stone Company and conversion works began in 1936. It was a

*Munitions train entering Tunnel Quarry via a branch line from the eastern end of Box Tunnel, 1940s*

colossal task. Two million tons of stone debris had to be removed, not to mention acres of malodorous manure from old mushroom beds. The whole 45-acre labyrinth had to be supported, reinforced and bomb-proofed. Air conditioning and safety shafts were installed and the quarry was supplied with its own power station.

To carry out the work, thousands of civilian workers were drafted in from

*Above: RAF bomb stores at Eastlays Quarry*
*Below: a vast arsenal of shells in Tunnel Quarry*

depressed areas such as South Wales, Durham and Cumberland. A vast influx of men and machinery caused consternation in the small rural communities around Corsham. The authorities made a doomed attempt at secrecy, attempting to maintain that the men had been drafted in to construct food dumps. Nobody was fooled. The workers were paid good wages, and after a few drinks on pay day, they were only too willing to discuss the real nature of their work. Understandably, there were occasional bouts of drunkenness, but these were severely stamped upon. Sentencing two workmen for brawling in 1938, the chairman of the magistrates declared: "When they come to

a place like Bath they should behave as Bath people behave. Bath people do not get drunk."

By 1938, work was well advanced on the underground arsenals and bombs, shells and other ammunition started to arrive at Tunnel Quarry and two smaller quarries nearby—Eastlays and Monkton Farleigh—which together comprised the Central Ammunition Depot (CAD) at Corsham. Throughout the war, CAD held over 300,000 tons of explosives at any one time. Thousands of people—service and civilian—worked underground, and Tunnel Quarry was supplied with offices, an important military telephone exchange, medical rooms, canteens and a chaplain's office. There were also barracks for 300 soldiers, but in the event these were seldom used except, oddly enough, by the Women's Auxiliary Air Force.

The WAAFs worked in Brown's Quarry, a small off-shoot of Tunnel Quarry. In 1940, this was converted into a

*Underground RAF control room in Brown's Quarry*

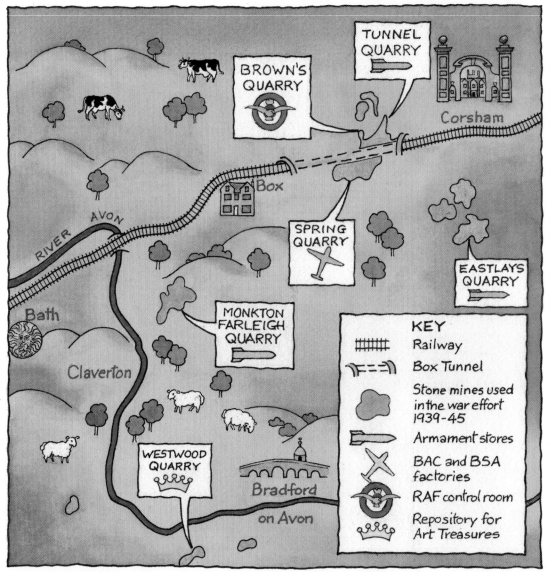

secure underground control centre for No. 10 Group, RAF Fighter Command, which was based above ground in nearby Rudloe Manor. This underground facility, constructed at enormous expense, centred on a classic operations room, as featured in innumerable wartime films. Measuring 50 foot/15 metres square, it had a huge plotting table at ground level, overlooked by glass-fronted booths for the controllers and radio operators. The walls were painted in a special scheme specified by the RAF, shading slowly from Goblin Green at the bottom to Primrose Yellow at the top, the theory being that this background would not distract the

*This page: large amounts of equipment—such as the massive generator (above), and the conveyor system leading to the surface (below)—still exist in Tunnel Quarry*

women operating the plotting table. If any flighty young WAAF was tempted to drift off into fantasies of pre-war shopping in Knightsbridge, she would feel perfectly at home in the electric lift which provided access to Brown's Quarry. This was reputedly commandeered from Harrods when a new one could not be acquired at short notice.

1940 was a dark and desperate time for Britain. In the spring, the British Expeditionary Force was forced to retreat from France at Dunkirk, leaving the whole French coast in German hands. Invasion was no longer just a

possibility—it was expected any day. The Corsham Garrison was on full alert and reinforcements arrived to protect the priceless underground stores. Ammunition shipped back from France arrived at Monkton Farleigh Quarry for sorting. Inspectors found a strange rag-bag crammed into the crates. Slipped in between the shells, there were hundreds of letters written to loved ones by soldiers of the BEF who feared they would never find their way home.

In the fields around Corsham, decoy lights were set up to deflect night-time bombers from their real targets. The depots were bomb-proof, but the railway connections on which they depended were very vulnerable. The decoy light systems were highly sophisticated. Following warning of an attack, lighting would be turned on to simulate the pattern the enemy would expect to see at the real target. The lights would then be shut off after a slight delay, leaving just a few small lights to simulate an incomplete, emergency blackout.

Happily, the Corsham area escaped relatively unscathed in the event. Bristol was not so lucky. The City held prime targets for the Luftwaffe, not least the Bristol Aircraft Company (BAC) in Filton. In September 1940 the BAC works suffered two devastating attacks which killed 160 people and seriously disrupted production. Throughout the autumn, bombing continued relentlessly on other centres of arms and aircraft manufacture in Southampton, Birmingham and Coventry. In response, Lord Beaverbrook, Minister of Aircraft Production, pushed forward emergency plans to transfer much of the aircraft industry to great underground factories. The largest of these was constructed in 90-acre Spring Quarry, which is situated on the south side of Box Tunnel.

Spring Quarry was still being mined, but in December 1940 it was peremptorily requisitioned from the Bath & Portland Stone Company. Quarrymen were ordered to down tools and leave on the spot. In the far reaches of the quarry, some of these tools still lie where they were dropped.

10,000 Irish labourers were recruited in Dublin to carry out the Herculean (and hideously expensive) task of converting the quarry into underground factories for the Bristol Aircraft Company's engine development department and production line, and for the Birmingham Small Arms Company (BSA) which produced, amongst other arms, the machine guns for Spitfires and Hurricanes.

Unlike the ammunition depots, which had been planned and prepared before the war started, the underground factories were built in a state of near panic. Hastily-laid plans had to be changed time and again, completion dates kept slipping back and costs spiralled out of control.

The Treasury became increasingly concerned and tempers rose. Government departments locked horns with BAC and BSA on almost every subject. Even the decor of the BAC workers' canteen caused heated debate. Sir Reginald Verdon Smith, chairman of BAC, eventually prevailed, and he commissioned Olga Lehmann, a well-known set designer, to cover the canteen walls in spectacular murals, many of which survive to this day. The style is exuberant in the extreme, and subjects range from dinosaurs to Ascot race meetings. Lehmann was assisted by Gilbert Wood, a riotous, hard-drinking individual with a hatred for clergymen. One of his most startling tableaux depicts a group of cannibals boiling a missionary in a large black pot.

Eventually, it was late in 1942 before BAC and BSA moved into Spring Quarry. By this time, the threat of invasion had passed and German bombing had greatly reduced. In retrospect, the underground factories were virtually redundant by the time they were occupied, but at the time no-one could be sure what was to come. Winston Churchill himself was a vehement champion of underground citadels, and the policy forged ahead. In the event, the Spring Quarry factories made a real—albeit very expensive—contribution to the war effort and it was here that BAC developed and produced the famous Centaurus engine. In the later stages of the war, the supremely light and powerful Centaurus was the force behind the Hawker Typhoon, Tempest and Sea Fury.

The Spring Quarry factories were wound up early in 1945, but a few miles away at Westwood Quarry, near Bradford on Avon, underground production continued far longer. The Royal Enfield Cycle Company began producing anti-aircraft and radar equipment there in 1942, and continued to use the site both for defence contracts and for its core motorcycle business right up until 1970.

Behind Royal Enfield's wartime production line, deep in the far reaches of Westwood Quarry, lay a fabulous treasure house. Here, many of the most valuable objects from the V&A, the British Museum and other collections were brought to protect them from bombing and looting. They were kept in tunnels specially converted to provide the ideal temperature and humidity to preserve priceless antiquities, tapestries, sculptures and metalwork. The Elgin Marbles and the Crown Jewels were just some of the unique treasures which sat out the war under the fields of Wiltshire.

In 1945 war ended in Europe and the Far East, but the peace was fragile and east-west relations deteriorated rapidly.

*Olga Lehmann's cheery barmaids in the BAC canteen in Spring Quarry*

Photos on pages 63–65 courtesy of Sir George White

Successive British governments believed that armament levels should be maintained, and the underground arsenals around Corsham continued in service right through the 1950s. Eventually, however, the increasing importance of nuclear power made conventional weapons seem obsolete, and stocks were run down. In the early 1960s, the area around Monkton Farleigh was frequently rocked by thunderous explosions as huge amounts of ammunition were detonated in demolition pits.

The nuclear age brought a new role for the old factories in Spring Quarry. Within two years of the end of the war,

**This page: The Spring Quarry murals are still in an excellent state of preservation—despite the damp**

the area appears to have been earmarked as a refuge for central government in the event of attack by atomic—and later nuclear—bombs. It was an ideal site: a ready-made underground complex, deep enough to be virtually blast- and radiation-proof, and offering many essential services. Some form of emergency headquarters seems to have been planned as early as 1947, when access to Spring Quarry was severely restricted as "the future use of the site may be somewhat sensitive".

In the 1950s, as the Cold War grew chillier, preparations for a Central Government War Headquarters at Spring Quarry were taken further. As well as highly sophisticated communications equipment, the quarry was provided with dormitories, dining rooms, kitchens and a huge fresh-water lagoon to serve several thousand people, including the Prime Minister and War Cabinet. Facilities included a licensed bar.

The emergency nuclear HQ at Corsham, code-named "Burlington", continued to be maintained throughout the 1960s and 1970s. Then, in the early years of Margaret Thatcher's government, it underwent major upgrading as part of a new, aggressive approach to civil defence. These preparations were officially secret, but rumours abounded. The public saw nuclear bunkers as a cynical attempt by the Establishment to save their own skins, and attitudes hardened.

Around Corsham, local people became increasingly suspicious of the "Caves of Death". Feelings ran high when (unfounded) rumours began to circulate that one of the quarries was being prepared as a shelter for the Royal Family. In 1981, locals were further outraged when a developer purchased Eastlays Quarry and set about transforming it into a "nuclear condominium", intended to provide 10,000 wealthy people with protection against thermonuclear war. While the outside world vaporised in the holocaust, the lucky inhabitants would enjoy life in luxury suites, served by shops, cinemas and sports facilities. In the event, the developers went bankrupt and the would-be nuclear survivors lost their £8,000 deposits.

*Spring Quarry was a fully-equipped underground city*

Since the 1980s, the Government has divested itself of most of its underground sites around Corsham. Several of the quarries are now used by commercial companies for secure storage. At Eastlays, wine bottles are laid down where TNT used to be stacked. However, there is little doubt that the Ministry of Defence still actively maintains strongholds capable of protecting key government and military personnel in the event of attack from a "rogue" state. Tunnel Quarry remains in MoD hands, and may yet be called back into active service.

## want to know more?

### Britain's Underground Defences:

The full story of Britain's underground defence network can be found in *Secret Underground Cities* by N.J. McCamley, published by Pen & Sword Books Ltd. We would like to thank Nick McCamley for all his generous help.

# Bringing the

The village of Combe Down on the outskirts of Bath is a delightful spot. With its winding lanes, picturesque cottages and old-fashioned shops, it appears peaceful and timeless—as safe as houses. There is only one peculiar feature: an over-zealous traffic official seems to have been let

loose in the area. Closed roads, weight restrictions and "No Waiting" areas abound. On the surface, it all seems quite unnecessary—but drivers are well-advised to heed the warnings. Less than 6 foot/2 metres below some busy roads, there are sheer drops into old stone mines.

Large parts of the village are "floating" above massive caverns. There are fears of subsidence and even collapse where the

mine roofs are known to be particularly thin. Householders are finding it difficult to get insurance and uncertainty overshadows the property market. The mines must be stabilised and various proposals are being put forward, but opinions differ on the best solution, and the issue has divided local residents. Adding fuel to the fire, one of Britain's rarest bats has established a colony in the mines.

The Georgian City of Bath was built from the stone quarried and mined from Combe Down. This was the source of "Bath stone"—the honey-coloured oolitic limestone that was used in the construction of so many buildings. Small-scale quarrying has probably been going on since Roman times in the Combe Down area, and there are remains of a Roman villa on the south side of the village. It was not until the eighteenth century, when Bath became the most fashionable resort in England, that stone was extracted in huge quantities. Stone that could be quarried from surface outcrops quickly ran out, so mines were driven deeper and deeper into the hillsides of Combe Down.

Three men orchestrated the transformation of Georgian Bath—Beau

# house down

Nash, the ebullient Master of Ceremonies, architect John Wood and entrepreneur Ralph Allen. Wood and Allen planned a complete rebuilding of Bath, and to gain access to the high quality stone they needed, Allen began to purchase the land around Combe Down in 1726. By 1744 he owned the whole area and had created a highly successful, integrated stone business incorporating many technical innovations. These included an inclined railway which used gravity to draw trucks laden with massive blocks of stone from the mines

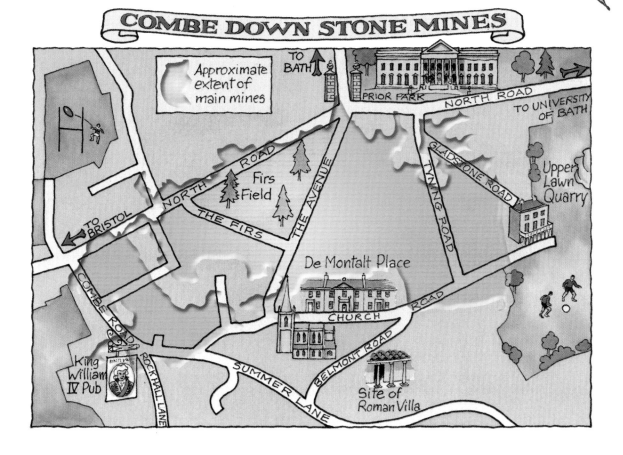

COMBE DOWN STONE MINES

*This page: Prior Park Mansion (above) and the Palladian Bridge (below)*

down to the River Avon one and a half miles away at Widcombe, and thence to markets in Bath, Bristol and beyond.

Ralph Allen was a man of extraordinary vision and drive. He came to Bath from Cornwall at the age of 17 to take up a humble job as assistant to the postmaster, but within a few years he had revolutionised the whole postal service and made a fortune. Allen applied the same flair at Combe Down. He was a shrewd publicist and managed to create a wide market for Bath stone and transform its reputation. Hitherto, it had been considered inferior to Portland stone, which is harder, but Allen harnessed the glamour of spa society to give Bath stone a stylish new image.

Prior Park, the imposing mansion that Allen built for himself at Combe Down, was designed as an advertisement for his product. It has a long, porticoed façade and is set in glorious landscaped gardens complete with a Palladian bridge—built of Bath stone, naturally. Here, Allen entertained the

*De Montalt Place (above and left)*

brightest and the best from every field, including Thomas Gainsborough, Frederick Handel and Henry Fielding. Fielding immortalised his genial host as Squire Allworthy in *Tom Jones*.

By the standards of the time, Ralph Allen was a caring and honourable

employer. He showed genuine concern for the safety of his labour force and offered fair wages and good working conditions. Several of the sturdy cottages he built for his masons survive in the village, including the row now known as De Montalt Place.

Lavish entertainment and generous treatment of his workers did little for

*One of the mine "tramways" (main access roads)*

69

*Above: evidence of an earlier attempt to shore up the mines*
*Below: several villagers have mine entrances in their gardens*

Allen's finances and he was heavily in debt by the time he died in 1764. His business empire quickly broke up and his land was acquired by various tenants. Quarrying continued, however, and the reputation of Bath stone went from strength to strength. The construction of the Kennet and Avon Canal in 1810 opened up even wider markets.

Phillip Nowell, who ran the Byfield mine (under the west side of the present village) was contracted to provide stone for Longleat, seat of the Marquis of Bath. The results seem to have impressed King William IV, and he commissioned Nowell to carry out work on Windsor Castle and then on his new London home—Buckingham Palace. Apart from the well-known frontage to the Mall, which is faced with Portland stone, most of the Palace, including the garden frontage, was constructed from Combe Down stone, and was completed in 1834. Phillip Nowell was knighted for his work, and in celebration, the beerhouse he built for his workers was renamed the King William IV, and so it remains.

*A Common Bat, roosting in the mines*

The Buckingham Palace project marked the high point of stone mining in Combe Down. In the middle years of the nineteenth century, less and less stone was extracted, and by the 1860s major underground workings had ceased. A few small surface quarries continued and one—Upper Lawn Quarry, which lies to the east of the village—is still in operation today.

Stone mining may have declined in the nineteenth century, but Combe Down got a new lease of life from another source. The area's sunny, south facing slopes and clean air were considered ideal for convalescents and sensitive folk who preferred to avoid the noise, pollution and scandalous fleshpots of central Bath. There was a boom in building detached villas and "gentlemen's residences" and the area became a magnet for retired military officers and clergymen. By 1900, Combe Down had transformed from an industrial village into a prosperous suburb.

Beneath this solid and respectable surface, however, the old stone mines were on the move. Natural fractures in the rock mean that, over time, the roofs of the mines have a tendency to sheer away in layers, so that the distance between the mine ceilings and the buildings and roads above them gets thinner and thinner. In more recent years, vibration from traffic has accelerated this problem, and rock falls are common. About 30% of the mines have now suffered major roof collapse. In some places the ceilings of the mines are now so near the surface that the rumble of traffic can clearly be heard underground.

Another problem has been caused by "pillar robbing". The old quarrymen left pillars of stone to hold up the roof as they drove workings further and further into the hillsides. In later years, local people came and went as they pleased in the abandoned mines and helped themselves to building stone. They chose the easiest places to hack it out—and unfortunately, this was usually from the lower part of pillars. This went on until quite recent times, and some of the pillars are now so spindly at the base that they are in danger of collapse.

And it doesn't stop there. Over the whole Combe Down area, there are around 60 shafts leading from the mines to the surface, originally built to allow light and air to enter, and stone to be hauled out. Most of these were later capped with masonry or backfilled with debris tipped from the surface, but many of them are weak points.

*A perfect example of "pillar robbing"*

the wide underground access roads (known as tramways) which the quarrymen had hacked out are still intact. But in other places, the way is blocked by piles of waste rock or by collapsed mine roofs. Some of the surface shafts, which were used as rubbish tips until a few years ago, provide some very unappetising obstacles in the form of putrefying waste.

The doughty surveyors ploughed on, sometimes cramming themselves through tiny spaces to reach the more remote areas. They managed to map 40 acres of the mines, although there were further areas which were completely inaccessible to them. Some of these caverns have been detected by boring exploratory holes from above ground, but the full extent of the mines is still not entirely certain.

One thing is crystal clear—the mines need stabilising urgently. In response to the survey in 1993, the Council's first proposal was to fill up huge areas of the mine complex with pulverised coal ash from power stations, mixed with cement and pumped into the

In the early 1990s, several unnerving incidents with these shafts prompted Bath and North East Somerset Council (B&NES) to commission a full survey of the mines. This was no easy task. In parts

*Above: A young Horseshoe Bat*
*Below: Crumbling pillars destabilise the mines*

voids. This suggestion sparked off fierce debate and divided the community. Some people were adamant that the village should be made safe by any practical means, as quickly as possible. Others argued passionately that the historic mines should not be destroyed wholesale and that Combe Down's heritage must be preserved.

To complicate matters still further, the mines have become a unique sanctuary for thousands of bats. Of the 14 species of bat indigenous to Britain, seven use the mines. These include the Greater Horseshoe Bat—a very rare species of which there are probably only about 4,000 individuals in the whole country. Every autumn these bats—which can live for up to 30 years—return to the same places to hibernate. In early summer, the females return again to form "maternity colonies" and give birth to their single young. All species of bat are protected by law and disruption of their traditional roosts would unquestionably have a dire effect, especially on the precious colony of Horseshoes.

Nevertheless, 700 human homes are in danger and the fragile state of the mines cannot be ignored. Many roads are closed or have restricted access and emergency work is under way. Miners from South Wales and the Forest of Dean have been recruited to build secure timber walkways and prop up danger points, including the notorious

"Sector X". This area was not discovered by the 1993 survey, but was later located by boreholes. When an entrance was opened up, it was found to be in an alarming condition. The sagging roof was on the point of collapse and passing traffic could have been swallowed up at any moment. Thankfully, Sector X was discovered in time and was rapidly reinforced and made safe.

A permanent stabilisation plan for the whole mine complex is still some way off. The Council has set up a special project team which is working hard to reconcile conflicting local opinions and develop a solution that will satisfy everyone. One suggestion is to build a series of support pillars—but it would require a staggering 40-50,000 of these to make such a large area safe. Some people have put forward the rather startling idea of moving all 700 houses affected and collapsing the mines.

Somewhat less sensational proposals include filling up large areas with foam concrete, but there is no going back from such a course—mines filled in this way would be gone forever. Many residents prefer the option of filling with sand or limestone gravel, which leaves open the possibility of removing the infill at some future date. At the same time as all these options (and others) are being considered, a substantial group of residents are campaigning for a Heritage Centre with access to parts of the mines and CCTV which would allow visitors to watch the bats.

The public consultation process continues and around £40 million has been earmarked for the massive works involved. There is a long way to go, but it is hoped that the end result will preserve part of the historic mine network, protect wildlife and allow residents to sleep easy in the knowledge that their homes will still be above ground in the morning.

*Left: The mines are 26 feet/8 metres deep in places*
*Below: Reinforcements in "Sector X"*

# River of

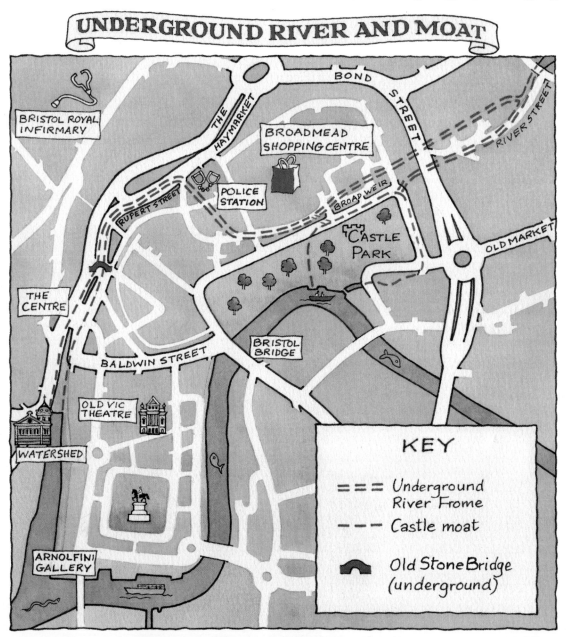

UNDERGROUND RIVER AND MOAT

BRISTOL ROYAL INFIRMARY

BOND STREET

RIVER STREET

BROADMEAD SHOPPING CENTRE

THE HAYMARKET

RUPERT STREET

POLICE STATION

BROAD WEIR

CASTLE PARK

OLD MARKET

THE CENTRE

BALDWIN STREET

BRISTOL BRIDGE

OLD VIC THEATRE

WATERSHED

ARNOLFINI GALLERY

**KEY**

=== Underground River Frome

--- Castle moat

Old Stone Bridge (underground)

# darkness

A ny Wednesday, you may witness surreal scenes outside Westgate, the office building at the northern end of the Centre. Suddenly, rubber-clad men may emerge from under the ground bearing strange objects—an uprooted tree perhaps, or a sodden three-piece suite. These men are sanitary officials, who go down every week to inspect and clear the River Frome, which runs unseen for well over a mile beneath the streets of Bristol, from the Watershed at the southern end of the Centre to Wade Street in St. Paul's.

Bristol's second river wasn't always invisible. It once flowed fair and brisk (for that is what its name means) through the City and into the River Avon. But over the years, Bristolians have forced the Frome to adapt to their changing needs. They have altered its course, blocked it up here and channelled it off there, used it as a defence, a harbour and a sewer, and finally, when it became a nuisance, they buried it. The history of the Frome is a miniature history of Bristol.

*Reconstruction of Bristol Castle, c. 1310. On the left is the River Frome which feeds water into the moat*

*Impression of the castle moat c. 1350 by Christine Molan*

The river rises near Tetbury in Gloucestershire and flows into Bristol from the north through Frenchay, Stapleton and Eastville to St. Paul's, where it disappears from view. From here it flows underground along River Street, around the north of Castle Park, on to Bridewell Police Station, and down Rupert Street to Westgate. Finally, it runs under the Centre and out into the Floating Harbour by the Watershed, but the original course of this last stretch of the Frome was different. It followed the line of St. Stephen's Street and Baldwin Street, joining the Avon near Bristol Bridge. Just before they converged at this point, the Frome and the Avon flowed close together. The narrow strip of land in between was easy to defend and well-placed to control a natural crossing-point of the Avon. It was here that the Saxon settlement of Bricgstow ("place by the bridge") grew up, and this

78

area remained the walled heart of the City for centuries.

William the Conqueror quickly recognised the strategic importance of Bristol, and sent Geoffrey of Mowbray to take charge of the town. He built a simple fortification which his successor, Robert of Gloucester, transformed into a huge castle that grew to be twice the size of Caernarvon Castle and one of the grandest in the kingdom. It was built to the east of the town, between the Frome and the Avon, thus closing off the only access by land.

The castle consisted of a massive stone keep and numerous other buildings including stables, a chapel and a fine banqueting hall, all enclosed by great stone walls—and, of course, a moat. To form this, water from the Frome was fed through weirs around the castle walls and out into the Avon via a great water gate. This meant that Bristol was completely encircled by the two rivers and, as one medieval writer put it, seemed to be "swimming in the water".

Bristol Castle had a rather strange history. At first, the grim royal stronghold dominated the medieval town, but when the powerful merchant classes began to throw off feudal control, the castle's influence waned. By the sixteenth century it had fallen into disrepair and disrepute. The castle precinct was still Crown property and the Bristol justices had no power over it, so it became a refuge for outlaws. Within the crumbling walls, all manner of "robbers, malefactors and other inordinate livers" squatted in cramped hovels. This sordid den was a thorn in the side of the City fathers, and they longed to get their hands on the valuable site and redevelop it.

At last, in 1630, the City succeeded in buying the castle, but before they had a chance to do much with it, the Civil War broke out and the castle was re-fortified for active service. Bristol came out on the Parliamentary side, but the Royalists seized and held the City for a while. This was a bitter blow to Cromwell, and may be what prompted him to draw Bristol's teeth in 1654 by ordering that the castle be dismantled. The City Council was delighted, and set about the task with a will.

**Bristol's ducking-stool plunged "nagging women" into the castle moat**

*Above: Entrance to the sally port in Castle Park*
*Below: The sally port in use; illustration by Christine Molan*

Every citizen was ordered to donate one day's labour a week, and within a few months the great fortress was no more. The area was rebuilt as Bristol's main shopping centre, and thus it remained until the Luftwaffe's incendiary bombs destroyed it in November 1940.

The bomb site has now been turned into Castle Park. Above ground there is very little evidence of the castle—only some remnants of the banqueting hall and a few fragments of masonry from the keep and the round tower. Below ground, however, part of the castle remains almost intact—the moat. It has been covered over since 1847, but it is still there, is still part of the Frome water system and is still navigable by boat.

The moat is impressively wide and deep—as you can see from the last section of it, which emerges from a brick arch near the Ambulance Station to join the Floating Harbour. From here its course runs underground all the way round the south, east and north sides of Castle Park. The street called Broad Weir is directly over the moat, and if you stand at the bus stop, there may well be men working in the culvert beneath your feet. This section is currently being reinforced to prevent the road above from collapsing under the weight of laden double-deckers and depositing passengers into the moat below.

To the north of the moat are the weirs that feed water into the moat from the Frome. Here stood the castle mill, and the marks made by the great mill wheel can still be seen in the walls of the ancient mill tail which drove it.

The millpond area of the moat was the site of the City's ducking-stool from about 1552. This barbaric punishment for nagging women came to an abrupt halt in 1718 when a Mrs. Blake got her own back on Edmund

*St. Augustine's Parade, c. 1825. Painting by Samuel Jackson*

Mountjoy, the Mayor who had decreed her punishment. "If I'm a duck, then I'll make him pay for my dripping," she was heard to shout as she went under—and she was as good as her word. Mountjoy was sued for battery, and the damages awarded were so crippling that no official dared employ the stool's services again. An enterprising businessman made snuff-boxes out of the wood and marketed them on the promise that any man who used one would be relieved of his nagging wife forever. They sold like hot cakes.

The section of the moat to the west of the castle (facing the old town) is now a dry ditch—as it probably was for most of the castle's history. It can still be traced underground, and one entrance to it can be seen in Castle Park. Near the bombed shell of St. Peter's Church, there is a sunken metal grill, beyond which 27 steps lead steeply down into the moat. This was a sally port, through which defenders of the castle could "sally forth" and surprise any attackers who might be trying to undermine the walls.

Using the Frome to supply the castle moat (in the eleventh or twelfth century) was probably the first large-scale manipulation of the river, but soon afterwards the demands of commerce prompted an even more ambitious project. By the 1240s, Bristol had become a busy port and the harbour facilities were no longer adequate. So, at the gigantic cost of £5,000, the last stretch of the Frome was diverted from its original course. From Stone Bridge (near

Westgate) the River was channelled into a huge new trench which joined the Avon further downstream (near where the Arnolfini now stands). This provided a much bigger and better harbour, with plenty of new quays and loading bays. St. Augustine's Trench, or "Deep Ditch" as it was always known, became the heart of Bristol docks and one of the most famous sights in the City. As Alexander Pope wrote in 1739, "in the middle of the street as far as you can see, are hundreds of ships, their masts thick as they can stand by one another, which is the oddest and most surprising thing imaginable."

It sounds a prosperous and bustling scene, but there was one gigantic fly in the ointment. The Avon had a huge tidal range, as did the lower reaches of the Frome which flowed into it. At low water, ships in Bristol harbour sank precariously down into the mud, and Pope's forest of masts must have lurched crazily in all directions. Bristol's "soft and whosy harborow" (as one medieval commentator described it) became more and more hazardous and inconvenient as ships got bigger and trade got brisker.

By 1755, Bristol was the second largest port in the country—but was unlikely to retain this position. Disgruntled ship owners were tired of watching their craft expensively towed eight miles up the twisting, rocky Avon, only to break their backs on mud-banks in the harbour. More welcoming ports such as Liverpool

**An attempt to clean up the Floating Harbour, 1825. Painting by T. L. S. Rowbotham**

were starting to filch Bristol's trade, so in 1809, after decades of torpor and procrastination, the Floating Harbour was at last constructed. The beds of the Avon and Frome between Cumberland Basin and Totterdown Lock were sealed off from the tide so that the water level remained constant and ships could float at all times. The Avon itself was diverted through the New Cut—an artificial channel dug to the south of the City.

This solved one problem but caused another. The Frome had long been used as a dumping-point for sewage and rubbish, but the worst of it used to be swept away by vigorous tides into the Avon and, eventually, the sea. Now that the Frome was cut off from the tide, waste just collected on the river's banks, or drained into the stagnant Floating Harbour and festered. The stench was intolerable and the death rate soared, so in 1825 the Frome was once again diverted. At Stone Bridge (near Westgate) lock gates were constructed and the main flow of the Frome was taken through a new underground channel called Mylne's Culvert out to the tidal Avon at the New Cut.

This did nothing for the water quality of the New Cut, of course, but local people made the best of things. The mothers of Bedminster developed an interesting theory that a child with whooping-cough should be well wrapped up and

*The old Stone Bridge and River Frome under Westgate*

then pushed along the New Cut at ebb tide. They reasoned that the combination of the smell of rotting sewage and the pull of the tide would draw the illness from the child. There are well-attested cases of this treatment being administered as late as 1900.

Mylne's Culvert still regulates the Frome, and the old lock gates were still in service until a few years ago. Now they have been replaced by a new concrete weir which can be found, together with the old Stone Bridge itself, under the manhole covers by Westgate.

The Frome was open all along its length until 1858. By then, a winding river crossed by 13 bridges, some of them medieval, was starting to get in the way of the traffic. So bit by bit over the second half of the nineteenth century, the Frome was covered over with great brick culverts from Wade Street in St. Paul's to Stone Bridge. Several modern thoroughfares, such as

83

*Still on the waterfront: the Hippodrome c. 1930 (at that time devoted to the new talking pictures)*

Rupert Street and Fairfax Street, are built directly over the Frome culvert.

St. Augustine's Trench (under the Centre) was the last stretch to disappear. Part of it, from Stone Bridge to the Draw Bridge (near the end of Baldwin Street), was covered over to make a site for the 1893 Exhibition and subsequently the Tramway Centre. The rest of the historic Trench was still open until 1938, and it

remained a busy harbour, although the new docks at Avonmouth and Portishead were taking more and more shipping away from the centre of Bristol. It is strange to think that ships were moored in front of the Hippodrome when it opened in 1912. Appropriately, the first production was an "amazing water spectacle" entitled *Sands o' Dee* "in which enormous waves break across the seashore and horses dive into 100,000 gallons of water to the rescue of the heroine". The vast underfloor tank in which such extravaganzas were staged has been filled in, but the dolphins, anchors and ships' figureheads which still decorate the theatre are a reminder that it was once a dockside music hall. This area of the Trench was covered over in 1938, and now only the last

**Dead Dog Boat**

84

*The swans have been evicted as the harbour in front of the Hippodrome is covered over in 1938*

stretch in front of the Watershed remains open.

The Frome and all the channels into which it has been forced over the years now form an eerie network of underground waterways beneath Bristol. It is possible to travel by inflatable boat all along the underground river, under several ancient bridges which have been incorporated into the culverts, and all the way round the castle moat. It is possible—but certainly not pleasant. The culverts are claustrophobic, smelly and attract debris like magnets. Everything from allotment sheds to 40-foot trees get washed down them. At one time, so many dead animals found their way into the system that a craft called "Dead Dog Boat" regularly went round to fish them

out. The boatman was paid six old pence per animal and made a good living until his boat was wrecked in a storm in the early 1960s.

In recent years, there has been a good deal of controversy about the hidden river. Many Bristolians feel that a gigantic roundabout is an unworthy "Centre" for their great city, and would like to see St. Augustine's Trench opened up again. The City Council went through a lengthy consultation process and there was widespread approval for the scheme, but it was finally abandoned for financial reasons. For the moment, the only water in the Centre is provided by a few unreliable little fountains. But the river is hidden, not lost, and may yet make a comeback to restore Bristol's maritime heart.

# Tunnels

Mysterious tunnels, curious caverns, bizarre underground legends … the Bristol area has them all in abundance. Subterranean oddities crop up in the most peculiar places, and every one has a tale to tell. Many of these stories are almost certainly myths, but there is genuine evidence for others. Here are just a few of the strangest.

*The Temple at Stancombe*

At Stancombe Park, mid-way between Wotton-under-Edge and Dursley, there are some very odd tunnels indeed—designed to protect a clergyman's love-nest from his prying wife. Stancombe is a lovely eighteenth-century house of modest size, surrounded by magical gardens. The landscape is lush and a little wild, full of surprises, and winding paths eventually lead to a series of dark, narrow

# of Love

tunnels. The entrance to the labyrinth is guarded by a massive stone dog, and as you grope your way through, you encounter a shell grotto and an Egyptian-style ice-house arched over with a whale's jawbone. When you emerge into the light, a breathtaking vista opens up—a perfect, miniature Doric temple rising out of a shimmering lake.

The temple and the tunnels which guard it were built around 1820 by the Reverend David Purnell-Edwards, then owner of Stancombe. He had wisely married a wealthy lady of stout proportions, but—legend has it—he fell in love with a gypsy girl and the

*Above: Topiary gorilla*
*Below left: One of the narrow tunnel portals*

temple was their trysting place. The wily vicar carefully designed the access tunnels to ensure they were too narrow for his portly wife to negotiate.

Luckily, Evelyn Waugh (no sylph himself) managed to get through them a century later to view the temple, which he describes in *Brideshead Revisited*. Stancombe Park so fired Waugh's imagination that he wrote this famous novel whilst staying at the house.

87

Stancombe is still a private home and the owner is an inspired gardener who continues in the folly tradition. She has built a delightful Millennium Folly of doves and columns which blends in perfectly, and when she comes across an overgrown bush, she clips it into an animal shape. Her gorilla is particularly fine (even though it was recently converted from an unsatisfactory chicken). Honeymooners sometimes stay at the temple, which has been beautifully restored, but the only permanent residents are two cats—called Vicar and Gypsy.

Another pair of lovers—Adam and Eve—are associated with a far more sinister site on the banks of the Avon at Ham Green near Pill. This is the area of

*Left: view over the lake from the tunnels*
*Right: looking towards the shell grotto*
*Below: The charming Millennium Folly*

*The Adam and Eve at Ham Green. The vertical nature of the riverbank here made this the perfect "Hung Road"*

the Avon known as Hung Road, because it was here that, at low tide, ships were literally hung by their masts from great iron rings set unto the river wall to prevent them keeling over.

Beside the Hung Road is a white building with two towers and a gate between. Marked on maps as "The Folly", this is more likely a water gate for nearby Ham Green House, built around 1710. Set either side of the gate are two statues of a man and a woman. They are so weathered now as to be almost indistinguishable, but they give the building its local name—the Adam and Eve.

Legend has it that the Adam and Eve was connected to Ham Green House by underground tunnel—and there are good reasons why this might be true, although no tunnel entrance is visible now. The whole Hung Road area was for centuries a den of smugglers, and the notorious river pilots were known as the Pill Sharks. There were certainly hiding places for contraband along the Hung Road, and a search by customs men in 1798 unearthed huge stocks of brandy and rum from various holes and tunnels. The Bright family of Ham Green House were respectable people—but this does not mean they would have frowned upon smuggling. All classes despised import taxes, and outwitting the excise men was an accepted sport.

The Brights were puzzling people. For generations they were known for kindness, philanthropy and pioneering medical work. They were also West Indian slave merchants and plantation owners who vehemently opposed the Abolition Act of 1833. This paradox between good works and hideous cruelty is perhaps reflected in the legends which have grown up around the family. From the Adam and Eve, they say, slaves were taken to the cellars at Ham Green House. Another persistent old story tells how the mistress of the house was found with her lover, and they were dragged down the tunnel and walled up in the Adam and Eve, one in each tower, and left to die.

Ham Green House took on yet more chilling associations 100 years ago, when it became part of a new isolation hospital for infectious diseases. To be "sent to Ham Green" was looked upon as a death sentence. In the early days, when the sick were transported here by boat, they probably disembarked at the Adam and Eve. In later years, nurses came here to sit in the sun (and flirt with the Shirehampton lads who would cluster on the opposite bank). In the 1920s, two nurses were swept away and drowned

in the wake of a passing ship, and ever since then land access to the Adam and Eve has been closed off. Now that Ham Green Hospital is closing and the area is being redeveloped, perhaps evidence of the infamous tunnel may come to light during building and restoration work.

Ham Green is not alone—there are "smugglers' tunnels" aplenty all over the Bristol area. A lot of these are probably

*The New Bristol Gaol and the Louisiana—connected by a hangman's tunnel?*

*The back of the Rummer in St Nicholas' Market—well connected to the Bank of England?*

obsolete drains, but some of the City's old dockside pubs may have the genuine article. Smuggling was a thriving Bristol industry for centuries and inn-keepers were in the thick of it. The Llandogger Trow certainly had tunnels leading to Welsh Back, and the remains of one of these was found when the pub was refurbished in 1962. Sadly, it had to be destroyed for work on the foundations.

The Louisiana pub, by the roundabout on Wapping Road, has an interesting tunnel. The entrance is now bricked up, but it reputedly runs to the site of the nearby New Bristol Gaol. The Louisiana used to be the residence of the Sheriff, and it was from here that the hangman would walk underground to the gaol on execution days, to avoid being lynched. An arch beside Cumberland Road is one of the few remains of the New Gaol, which was a victim of the Bristol riots in 1831. Enraged by the visit of a prominent opponent of the Reform Bill—which proposed giving more people the vote—

mobs rampaged through Bristol for three days and two nights. The New Gaol was stormed, all the prisoners were freed and if the hangman was on the premises, he must have beaten a hasty retreat through the tunnel!

A more recent pub story concerns the Rummer in All Saints Lane. Although much changed, this is an ancient inn with a history going back seven centuries. Some years ago (or so pub regulars assert) the landlord decided to investigate a blocked-up tunnel in his old cellars. He chipped away at layer after layer of brick and stone—it became an obsession. At last the day came when he broke through and saw a shaft of light. Delight turned to horror as he came eyeball-to-eyeball with an armed guard. He had broken into the vaults of the Bank of England. Since this startling event, the Rummer has changed hands and the landlord has moved on. So is this an urban legend? Officials at the Bank of England refuse to confirm the story—but they refuse to deny it, either.

Urban legends and conspiracy theories galore have grown up around another raft of underground features—Bristol's nuclear bunkers. Never designed to protect the general public, they have always been viewed with suspicion. Over the years, rumours have circulated that everyone from royalty to unpopular TV personalities have places ear-marked in these facilities. The truth is more prosaic.

The first wave of bunker-building occurred in the 1950s, when nuclear war was still regarded as survivable, like the Blitz, and bomb-proof civil defence control centres were constructed in Henleaze, Speedwell and Bedminster (this last still exists). In the early 1980s, when east-west tension increased alarmingly, there was a new flurry of preparation for nuclear war. Along with the infamous "Protect and Survive" leaflet (which advised citizens to make a shelter under the kitchen table), Margaret Thatcher's government issued orders that utility companies and local councils must prepare nuclear bomb-proof facilities to protect essential services and personnel. Many of these facilities survive under council offices, civic centres and even old people's homes. A particularly fine emergency bunker under the council offices in Thornbury is still intact, waiting for the Four Minute Warning.

The most sinister-looking of all the bunkers is the Bristol War Room, the creeper-clad top of which crouches behind a small trading estate at Flowers Hill, Brislington. This was built in 1954 as an emergency Regional Seat of Government for the whole of the South West. Here, key officials were to shelter in the event of atomic war with Russia, and attempt to restore some form of law and order in the aftermath. Later, the War Room became the County of Avon nuclear war HQ, until Avon declared itself "nuclear free" in 1982. Now, all Bristol's bunkers are more-or-less obsolete and, in retrospect, seem pathetically inadequate. The War Room has been locked up for 20 years and no-one has tidied up the debris of the last civil defence exercise in 1980.

*All that is to be seen above ground of the Bristol War Room at Flowers Hill, Brislington*

*photo courtesy Nick McCamley*

*Mother Pugsley's Well—inside and out*

On a more homely note, unique underground features can be found in perfectly ordinary back gardens. One of the most fascinating lurks behind a bed of gladioli in a small garden in Cotham. On the surface, it seems to be a rather unprepossessing concrete "wishing well", circa 1950. Look down it, however, and you can see ancient stonework and, far below, the waters of a famous healing spring. This is Mother Pugsley's Well, renowned for curing blindness and eye complaints. The spring's history goes back at least 700 years, but it was in the seventeenth century that "Mother Pugsley" made it famous. She was a beautiful young woman who married a Royalist officer called Pugsley during the Civil War. He was recalled to duty immediately after the ceremony and killed in action. His desolate widow buried him beside the ancient well, which was in the middle of a field in those days, and refused to leave his grave. For 55 years she continued to live beside the well, and became known as a wise and kindly woman who gave sage counsel and comfort to the afflicted. The spring's medicinal waters became even more potent by virtue of the "maiden widow's tears" that fell into them, and people travelled miles to seek healing and advice. When Mother Pugsley died at the age of 80, she was buried in her wedding dress beside her husband.

Another suburban surprise can be found in Fairfield Road, Montpelier, where young Sophia Davies has an underground den in the back garden.

*Sophia and her grotto*

Built into the terraced hillside, it is a beautifully constructed round chamber, with a barrel-vaulted roof and Gothic arched door and window. Old maps show that this garden used to belong to an older house a little down the street, built around 200 years ago. This house was one of the elegant villas constructed at the time when Montpelier, which up until then had been a rural area, was being developed as a fashionable resort with a suite of "Grand Pleasure Baths". It was the perfect place for social climbers to set up home, and a householder with pretensions might well have built a folly in his grounds. It seems likely that Sophia's den is, in fact, a perfect little Georgian grotto.

## access information stancombe park

**Stancombe Park:**

Stancombe is not generally open to the public, but the owner occasionally takes parties round by appointment. Write to: Mrs. G. Barlow, Stancombe Park, Near Dursley, Glos. GL11 6AU.
It is possible to rent the Stancombe temple for short stays. Contact Rural Retreats on 01386 701177.

# Flushed

Next time you step on an innocent-looking manhole cover, bear in mind that it may be all that stands between you and an enormous shaft, deeper than the Avon Gorge. When you walk down stolid suburban streets, remember that tunnels big enough to drive a bus through may run beneath your feet. And if you happen to have an allotment behind Horfield's Cranbrook Road, you may be interested to know that a vast tank of aircraft hangar proportions yawns beneath your vegetable patch.

This subterranean maze is a superb new drainage system, of which the City is

*Main Trunk Sewer from Black Rocks to the Sewage Treatment Works at Avonmouth*

# with pride

justifiably proud. It is, at last, conquering an ancient problem. Bristol has grappled with inadequate drainage for centuries and, as many Bristolians know only too well, it is not so long ago that the City was renowned for devastating floods and an unsavoury pong in summer.

The River Avon was the heart of the problem. Bristol lies in a basin, drained by the Avon and the smaller rivers and streams that feed it. The Avon has the second largest tidal range in the world, and when heavy rains coincided with an exceptionally high tide, storm water simply had nowhere to go. As the Avon was also the dumping-point for most of Bristol's sewage until 1964, the flood waters which regularly invaded the City were particularly unappetising.

The new drainage system—which, it is hoped, will solve the twin problems of foul water and storm water once and for all—has now been completed. But it has been a long time coming.

Flooding has been a danger from time immemorial, and the sewage problem became acute back in 1809, when the Floating Harbour was constructed. Before that, the Avon and its tributary, the Frome, were both tidal right through the City, and the daily ebb and flow were enough to carry away most of the waste produced by a small population. In medieval times, masonry

*Overhanging privies draining into the Frome c.1820*

culverts were built to drain sewage and rainwater from streets into the rivers, and these served the City well for hundreds of years. Some have even been connected to the modern drainage system and are still in use today.

All in all, early Bristol was a breath of fresh air compared with many English cities. Millerd's map of 1673 is fulsome in its praise: "There are no sincks yt. come from any houses into ye. streets, but all is conveyed underground rendering the Cittie exceeding sweet and delightsom."

Unfortunately, this fragrant state of affairs could not continue indefinitely. In 1673 the population of Bristol was only 20,000, but by 1800 this figure had more than trebled. The profusion of "blood, garbage, stinking meat, dogs, cats, etc." which found its way into the Frome and Avon was already turning the heart of the City into an open sewer. The construction of the Floating Harbour in 1809 made it into a cesspool. To compete with other ports, Bristol desperately needed a safe, tide-free harbour, so the bed of the Avon between Cumberland Basin and Totterdown Lock (and consequently the whole of the River Frome, which flowed into it) was sealed off from the tide. The

*Work on the Northern Foul Water Interceptor*

98

Avon itself was made to run through a huge new artificial channel—the New Cut. The stagnant waters of the Floating Harbour rapidly filled up with sewage and conditions in the City became hard to stomach.

The hot summer of 1825 brought matters to a head. The "stagnant mass of

Broadmead, 1882. Central Bristol used to flood regularly

putridity" in the Frome and the Floating Harbour prodded the unhappy citizens into action. They obtained an injunction against the Docks Company, compelling them to remedy the situation. The result was Mylne's Culvert (called after its designer, William Mylne). This underground channel was intended to restore tidal conditions to the Frome by diverting it away from the Floating Harbour into the tidal New Cut. The culvert runs from Stone Bridge (the northern end of the modern Centre) to the New Cut near Bathurst Basin.

Mylne's Culvert is a fine piece of engineering and it still controls the flow of the Frome. However, it didn't entirely solve the sewage problem. It partially restored tidal conditions to the Frome, but only the highest tides penetrated far enough to flush the reeking banks. The

Floating Harbour continued to fester, and it is estimated that, by the middle of the nineteenth century, 34 sewers were discharging 20,000 tons of solid matter into it every year. Life was becoming intolerable—and death ever more likely. Bristol had achieved the dubious distinction of being the third most unhealthy city in the country.

Dr. William Budd, physician to the Bristol Royal Infirmary, gave this graphic evidence to the Health of Towns Commission in 1845:

"Along the whole course of the stream (The Frome) is a source of noisome effluvia, which in the summer season sensibly poisoned the air for a long way round . . . Between St. Johns Bridge and the Bridge at the Quay-Head, the nuisance reaches its climax. Privies up and down the stream belonging to the

houses which abut upon it hang over a bank of mud the level of which is only swept at spring tide, or when the Frome is swollen by freshets. The state of things in the interval is too loathsome and disgusting to describe."

The streets were no better than the rivers, as sewer building had not kept pace with population. There weren't enough of them and many were badly constructed. Some unfortunate householders actually found themselves on the receiving end of sewers which ran backwards. Even on the rare occasions when efficient new sewers were provided, penny-pinching Bristolians were reluctant to pay for connection. No wonder poor Sir Henry de la Beche, who conducted a survey of Bristol in 1845, found the City nauseating. He was forced to stand at the end of alleyways and vomit while an iron-stomached colleague, Dr. Playfair, inspected the overflowing privies.

A raging cholera epidemic was the last straw. In 1848, the Council at last determined to clean up the City and formed a Sanitary Committee to do it. Over the next 15 years, district by district,

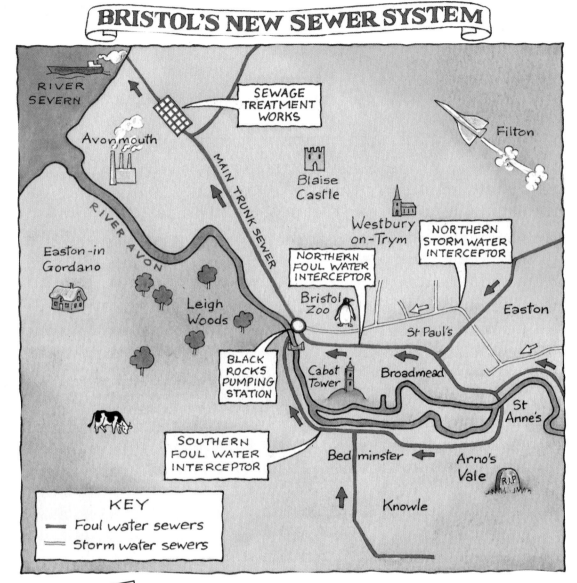

# BRISTOL'S NEW SEWER SYSTEM

RIVER SEVERN

Avonmouth

SEWAGE TREATMENT WORKS

MAIN TRUNK SEWER

Blaise Castle

Filton

Easton-in Gordano

RIVER AVON

Leigh Woods

Westbury on-Trym

NORTHERN FOUL WATER INTERCEPTOR

NORTHERN STORM WATER INTERCEPTOR

Bristol Zoo

Easton

BLACK ROCKS PUMPING STATION

Cabot Tower

St Paul's

Broadmead

St Anne's

SOUTHERN FOUL WATER INTERCEPTOR

Bedminster

Arno's Vale

R.I.P

Knowle

## KEY
— Foul water sewers
= Storm water sewers

they constructed 80 miles of sewers, which still form the bones of Bristol's drainage system. It was an impressive achievement. By 1869, *The Times* was able to report that Bristol had changed "from nearly the most unhealthy to nearly the most healthy town in Great Britain."

Although the Sanitary Committee solved the immediate problems, it was storing up more for the future. Their new system took sewage out of the streets and the Floating Harbour, but it still had to go somewhere—and unfortunately that somewhere was the tidal Avon, very near

the City. Bristol's waste continued to be dumped there right up until 1964, dosed by larger and larger quantities of chlorine as the City grew, the stench rose and the river died.

The expansion of Bristol increased the risk of flooding, too. Roofs and roads throw off water—unlike open land, which absorbs it and dissipates it slowly. So, in built-up areas, heavy rainfall fills streams and drains remarkably quickly— sometimes to overflowing.

By the end of the nineteenth century, it was clear that Bristol needed to solve her drainage problems once and for all, by getting storm water out of low-lying parts of the City and disposing of sewage safely.

The outlines of the modern system were first proposed in

*Above and below right: the Northern Storm Water Interceptor*

*Below: Celebrating the end of 17 months' tunnelling for the Southern Foul Water Interceptor*

1898, but turning the dream into reality took almost a century. The first proposal was rejected by a Town Meeting, even though it had been approved by the City Council. It was put forward again in 1905—and rejected again. Over the next 30 years, numerous committees, investigations and reports worried away at the problem without producing noticeable results. Then, just when it looked as though action was about to be taken, the Second World War intervened. At last, in 1959, construction of the present system began. In 1994—a full 96 years after the first proposal—the last link in the scheme (the Northern Foul Water Interceptor) was completed.

The new system is a marvel of engineering, but in essence it is beautifully simple. The foul water system consists of a ring of huge sewers which intercept all the smaller sewers around the City and take the waste to a main trunk sewer, which runs from Black Rocks Quarry to a sewage treatment works at Avonmouth. Here, effluent is treated and discharged into the Severn.

The storm water system simply diverts flood water away from low-lying parts of Bristol into enormous drains which discharge into the Avon, well away from the City Centre.

It all sounds straightforward enough, but the structures are breathtaking in scale and sophistication. Between Leigh Woods and Black Rocks Quarry, for example, there is a gigantic inverted siphon which draws sewage from the Southern Foul Water Interceptor and takes it 100 feet/30 metres beneath the bed of the Avon and up into the main Trunk Sewer on the other side.

Also near Black Rocks Quarry, the outfall of the Northern Storm Water Interceptor can be seen. This huge outfall is impressive enough, but it is nothing to what lies behind it. Out of sight, a horse-shoe shaped tunnel seven and a half miles long stretches away. It is around 16 feet/5 metres in diameter and up to 285 feet/85 metres below ground level in parts. Over

a quarter of a million cubic metres of rock and soil were excavated to make it, and it can cope with over three and a half million litres a minute.

Flows even greater than this can be controlled by detention tanks such as the one under the allotments behind Cranbrook Road in Horfield. This echoing vault with its rows of "Doric" pillars is like an eerie underground temple. It is huge—256 feet/77 metres long, 59 feet/18 metres wide and 21 feet/6 metres high—but normally contains a mere trickle of water. If there is a sudden surge, however, a hydrobrake swings into action, the tank fills up and the flow is released slowly to prevent flooding downstream in the centre of the City.

*The Cranbrook Road Detention Tank*

*The Malago Outfall: one of the huge drains that channel flood water into the Avon*

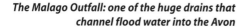

Even if 198,000 people decided to flush their lavatories at the same time, the detention tank could cope!

Size matters when in comes to sewers—at both ends of the scale. They not only have to deal with massive volumes, they also have to be so accurately laid that every millimetre counts. Bristol's sewage is conveyed down to Avonmouth by gravity, but to travel such a distance the gradient needs to

be extremely gentle—around 1 in 2,000. The tiniest miscalculation could spell disaster. All this had to be borne in mind by the heroic teams of men who worked for years in sweltering conditions under the City as they dug and blasted their way through rock which in places registered strengths ten times that of structural concrete.

It was a day of well-earned celebration when the last part of Bristol's new system—the Northern Foul Water Interceptor—was completed in 1994. On a special Open Day, 12,000 people took the opportunity to walk through part of the great tunnel before the first wave of sewage gushed through. This was the public's last chance to see the sewers, although they continue to hold a strange fascination. The authorities are bombarded with requests to visit or even hold functions in the system. Young lovers seem particularly sensitive to the romance of sewage, and many are keen to tie the knot in Bristol's watery underworld and sail off into married life on a rubber boat. Unfortunately, they can't. Most sewers are too dangerous for casual tourism. Poisonous gases, rats and disease are just a few of the risks. So perhaps it is best to stay on the surface and give thanks that these horrors have at last been banished to where they belong—the bowels of the earth.

*Open Day for the inauguration of the Northern Foul Water Interceptor, January 1994*

# Coal-Mines

# Proper

Deep in the ground beneath some of Bristol's most opulent buildings lies the foundation on which their prosperity was built: coal.

It is difficult to believe now, but Bristol was once a thriving mining area and rich veins of coal, honeycombed with mines, still run beneath the City. No other town in southern England has such a resource. It gave Bristol a unique advantage and was a key factor in the City's affluence and industrial growth, particularly in the seventeenth and eighteenth centuries.

# pit country

The Bristol and Somerset Coalfield is huge, running from Wickwar in the north to the Mendips in the south; from Clevedon in the west to Frome in the east. Unfortunately, the coal is difficult to extract because it occurs in thin seams, trapped between layers of rock. Eventually, this made the Bristol mines so unprofitable that they were all abandoned by the middle of the twentieth century.

*Above: pit ponies stayed underground all their lives*

*Left and below: Bristol miners spent whole shifts bent double in the narrow seams*

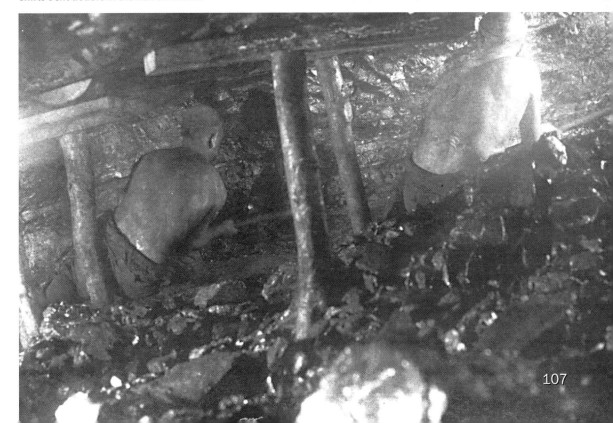

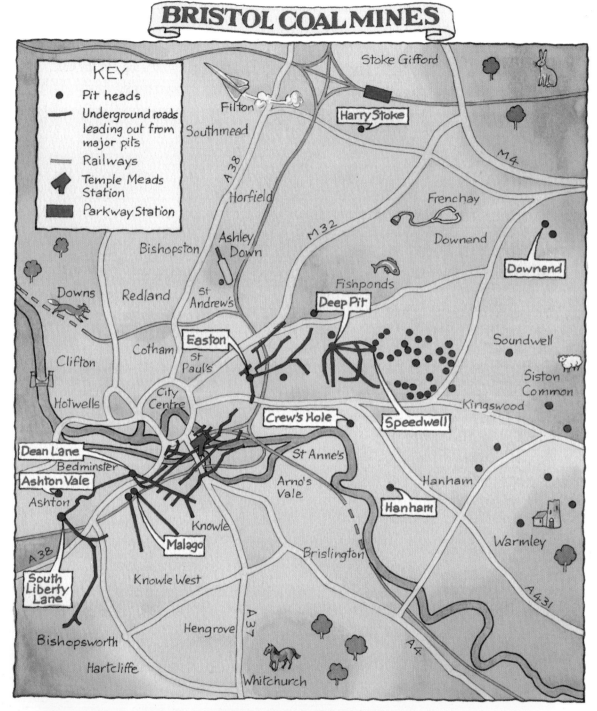

# BRISTOL COAL MINES

**KEY**

- • Pit heads
- — Underground roads leading out from major pits
- ═ Railways
- ◆ Temple Meads Station
- ▬ Parkway Station

*This map has been compiled from geological and historical plans and is not complete. For clarity, the mine workings are shown on top of the river, roads and railways. The numerous pitheads shown in east Bristol and the Kingswood district are just some of the large number of small, eighteenth century workings in the area. The pits with "underground roads" are the great Victorian collieries.*

Thin seams were no problem for Bristol's earliest miners because they only excavated coal which appeared near the surface or "cropped out". There are records of people harvesting coal in this way as far back as 1223, which makes Bristol one of the first coal-producing areas in the country. It was a small-scale operation in those days, with individuals or groups extracting modest amounts of coal for use in homes and the forges of local smiths. It wasn't until the sixteenth century, when demand for coal increased, that pits were dug and the pace of mining speeded up.

By the eighteenth century, more and more coal was needed to fuel Bristol's glass, china, sugar and metal industries. Between 1670 and 1750, the number of pits doubled in and around Kingswood, which was Bristol's principal mining area at that time.

The Kingswood miners were a law unto themselves. The area had been a Royal hunting ground—and on paper still was—but hordes of "squatters" had taken over wherever there was coal to be had. They were a turbulent crowd, and the Crown more or less gave up trying to control them.

They mainly worked small, shallow, bell-shaped pits, hacking out the coal and piling it into baskets which were then hauled out through a shaft to the surface. Three of these bell-pits were discovered recently by builders beneath the site of a new housing development in Warmley.

The miners lived a remote, primitive existence in scattered cottages and were considered little better than savages by their more civilised neighbours. Travellers gave the area a wide berth.

One man, however, made a bee-line for the lost souls of Kingswood. He was George Whitefield, a charismatic preacher and colleague of John Wesley's in the early days of the Methodist movement.

*South Liberty Lane Colliery, c. 1905, still surrounded by fields*

109

*Meal break c.1910. Miners ate little underground— heat and foul air killed their appetites*

On a bitter day in February 1739, he stood on Kingswood Common and, wild-eyed with emotion, delivered his message of hope to a crowd of astonished miners. Tears ran down their blackened faces. They were moved not only by his words and his obvious sincerity, but by the very fact that anyone should concern himself with outcasts such as they.

Others were not so impressed. *The Gentleman's Magazine* thundered: "The

industry of the inferior people in society is the great source of its prosperity. But if one man, like the Rev. Mr. Whitefield, should have it in his power, by his preaching, to detain five or six thousands of the vulgar from their daily labour, what a loss, in a little time, may this bring to the publick! For my part, I shall expect to hear of a prodigious rise in the price of coals about the city of Bristol, if this gentleman proceeds, as he has begun, with his charitable lectures to the colliers of Kingswood."

The well-to-do expected the masses to know their place and take their spiritual comfort from gin. Uplifting religion was as dangerous as education to the *status quo*, and the Methodists encountered outraged opposition. They were not intimidated, and John Wesley himself worked amongst the miners, organising a school for poor children and classes for adults. It was uphill work, but Kingswood became one of the first places in England where Methodism took root.

In the nineteenth century, coal-mining in Bristol reached the peak of its productivity and massive new collieries were developed in south and east Bristol. Modern, deep mining took over from small, shallow pits, and this meant the end of "independent" miners like the Kingswood tearaways, and the rise of powerful mining moguls. One of the

*A rare moment of relaxation. Like many miners, the man on the right worked almost naked*

*Dean Lane Colliery, c.1870s*

needs. Shafts were sunk deeper and deeper—as low as 1,464 feet/440 metres in the case of the aptly named Deep Pit in Kingswood—and workings fanned out for miles around these shafts. Tunnels were driven so far along seams that separate mines sometimes joined up. Workings from the south Bristol pits—situated around Ashton and Bedminster—extended right under the River Avon. In fact, the workings from Bedminster's Dean Lane Colliery passed beneath Redcliffe Caves and Temple Meads railway station and came within a few hundred yards of joining tunnels from Easton Colliery, although the pitheads were a full two miles apart. Large parts of central Bristol are built over a maze of exhausted workings, even though no shafts were ever dug there.

most attractive of these was a flamboyant character called Handel Cossham. He was a preacher turned colliery clerk and self-taught geologist of considerable talent. His contemporaries scoffed when he formulated scientific theories about the lie of the Bristol seams, but were forced to eat their words when he proved to be correct. Cossham's discoveries of fresh coal deposits made him an enormously rich man and Lord of the Manor of Kingswood.

In 1887, there were 17 pits in the Bristol field, employing about 2,500 underground workers and producing around half a million tons of coal a year. It was a small output compared with that of South Wales, but big enough to supply most of Bristol's

*Easton Colliery, c.1890. The miner's only light is the candle strapped to his head*

The geology of the Bristol coal seams meant particularly appalling conditions for the miners. Once they had been lowered by cage down the shaft, they often had miles to walk to the coal-face on which they were working—and they did not start earning until they got there. Until the 1890s, when lamps were introduced, a miner worked in total darkness apart from the light of a candle strapped to his hat. The seams were so narrow that men often had to work on their knees, or even on their backs, in a space which might be considerably less than 3 feet/l metre high. Boys were used in seams too narrow for grown men. Accident records from Easton show that boys as young as 12 were working—and dying—in the pits as late as 1889. Even when mechanical cutting equipment was developed, it was useless in such cramped conditions. Right to the end, most Bristol coal was hand-dug with pickaxe and shovel, and hauled to the bottom of the shaft by pony.

Ventilation was very poor in most pits, and many men stripped to a pair of shorts for work because of the unbearable heat. Worse still, gasses such as "firedamp" (methane) could build up, causing dreadful explosions. One such, which occurred at the Dean Lane Pit in 1886, killed ten men. Eight more were burnt or blinded. Half of these casualties were teenagers.

Flooding was another ever-present danger, and the death toll in the Bristol pits was high. Until well into the twentieth century, there was little hope of compensation for widows, orphans or the disabled, as most of the local pit-owners were less than

*This plaque was erected by Living Easton on the site of Easton Colliery, which is now an adventure playground. The panel on the left depicts a terrible explosion in the mine, which took many lives in 1886*

*A rare reminder of Bristol's mining past*

Tight-fisted owners, combined with low productivity, always kept wages low in the Bristol pits. In 1914, the average Bristol miner earned only 5s 6d (27p) a shift—one fifth lower than the national average.

In an effort to improve pay, safety and conditions, the Bristol pits were strongly unionised towards the end of the nineteenth century. A guiding light in this movement—and one of the most loved and respected men in Bristol's recent history—was Charlie Gill.

Mr. Gill was born in Bedminster in 1871. There were 14 mouths to feed in his family, so at the age of 11 he had to start

generous. Their attitude to fatal accidents is particularly revealing. As a mark of respect, the whole pit traditionally stopped work for 24 hours when a death occurred; in Bristol, that meant every man was docked a day's pay.

*The skateboard area in the Dame Emily Playpark, Bedminster, which stands on the site of the Dean Lane Colliery*

*One of the great undergound roads connecting the coal faces to the pithead at Easton*

earning. The only choice was to go down the pit and he worked underground for the next 31 years. In a small cottage, he raised seven children with his wife Florence, who supplemented the family income by sewing waistcoat buttonholes at one penny (0.4p) a time.

In many ways, his was the life of a typical Bristol miner, but Charlie Gill was no ordinary man. He had a passion for knowledge, and in his scarce spare time he studied for a local degree in mining at Technical College. His passion for justice was even greater, and he fought for the rights and welfare of miners and their families for 50 years. His intelligence and compassion won the respect even of his adversaries. In 1947, the former pit boy was elected Lord Mayor of Bristol and he was later awarded the MBE and CBE.

The unions gradually won improved conditions for the Bristol miners, but when it came to saving their jobs, they were fighting a rear-guard action. The thin seams of coal became more and more uneconomical to mine, and the Bristol pits simply could not compete with the Northern coalfields, where new coal-cutting machinery could be used on more accessible seams.

One by one, the pits closed—Malago Vale before 1900, Easton in 1911, Ashton Vale and Dean Lane by 1914, and the last works (at Speedwell) in 1936. There was a short flicker of revival at Harry Stoke in the 1950s with the opening of a modern drift mine (accessed by tunnelling back from outcrops on hillsides, rather than by deep shafts from the surface)—but it was finished by 1963. In north Somerset, mining continued a little longer, and it was not until 1973, when the Writhlington pit closed, that the very last coal was extracted from the ancient Bristol and Somerset Coalfield.

It is only a few decades since the Bristol mines closed, but it is almost as if they had never existed. There are no slag heaps because the Bristol colliers usually left waste underground and packed it into old workings as they advanced along the seams. All the Bristol pitheads have been demolished and even the sites are difficult to locate. It is hard to imagine, for instance, that the skateboard area in Bedminster's Dame Emily Playpark is over the Dean Lane pit shaft, scene of so much horror in 1886. Miners' cottages, too, are now hardly recognisable. They have been upgraded into desirable period properties, with the outside privies and tin baths long since replaced by modern bathrooms.

Pub names are one of the few enduring relics of Bristol's mining heritage. When you come across a Miners' Arms or Jolly Collier, you can be sure there was a pit nearby. This may well have been

where the miners were paid their wages, and is almost certainly where they spent a good deal of them at the end of a back-breaking, filthy week.

On the surface, centuries of hardship, drama and tragedy have scarcely left a trace. Underground, miles of dark, dripping tunnels will always remain as a memorial to the courage of the Bristol miners.

*Pit managers at South Liberty Lane*

# Middle-Age

Bristol was a medieval boom town. By the thirteenth century, it was one of the largest and richest cities in England. The port was doing a roaring trade, mainly importing wine and exporting wool and cloth, and the city was famous for huge fairs which attracted traders and entertainers from miles around. Thirteen flourishing monasteries and friaries encircled the city.

Above ground, churches are almost the sole survivors of this Golden Age. The flesh has gone from medieval Bristol—but underground, much of the skeleton remains. The city's support system was built below street level, and a good deal of it is still down there, working for a living. Great stone cellars, built to house hogsheads of wine in the thirteenth century, are still guarding precious vintages. Medieval culverts still form part of Bristol's drainage system, having outlived many later efforts. An ancient conduit still pipes spring water into the City Centre as it has for over 600 years, even during the worst days of 1940, when all the neighbouring water supplies had succumbed to enemy bombs.

This medieval underworld spreads out for miles under the streets of Bristol. Beneath Fosters Rooms in Small Street, for instance, there are fine medieval vaults which give access to a huge maze of cellars leading off in all directions as far as the law courts, the Grand Hotel, and beyond. Fosters was the home of John Foster, a fifteenth century Mayor

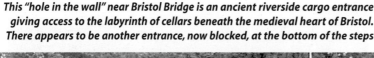

*This "hole in the wall" near Bristol Bridge is an ancient riverside cargo entrance giving access to the labyrinth of cellars beneath the medieval heart of Bristol. There appears to be another entrance, now blocked, at the bottom of the steps*

# Spread

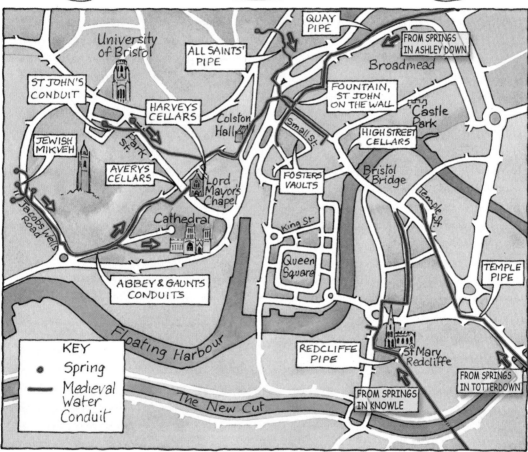

MEDIEVAL CELLARS & CONDUITS

of Bristol and a prosperous merchant who, like many of his kind, "lived over the shop". Houses had living quarters on the upper floors, business premises at street level and storage space beneath. More care and money was lavished on the cellar than any other part of the building, because its contents would usually be far more valuable than anything above ground. Most cellars were massively constructed from expensive stone, unlike the flimsy wooden houses which topped them. Fire swept through medieval towns so regularly that houses were almost

117

*This curious concrete obelisk on High Street (above) is the entrance to magnificent medieval cellars (below)*

thought of as disposable items, whilst their cellars were designed to outlive them.

The whole of central Bristol used to be honeycombed with such cellars. William Wyrecestre, a fifteenth-century surveyor who spent years painstakingly measuring and describing every building in Bristol, records unbroken chains of them beneath the houses of street after street. Many extended right out under the road, and for a long period wheeled traffic was banned from the busiest thoroughfares in case they collapsed under the weight. It was probably an unnecessary precaution—these cellars were built to last, and many survived direct hits in the Blitz. Several still exist under the Castle Park area, although the buildings above them were destroyed by the Luftwaffe. Beneath a peculiar concrete "obelisk" in High Street, for example, are some of the finest medieval cellars in Britain, with beautiful rib-vaulted ceilings which would not disgrace a Gothic cathedral. These cellars are not open to the public, unfortunately, but many others are, particularly in Small Street and Corn Street, where a number of medieval vaults are still in active service as restaurants, clubs and storerooms.

Some cellars still house wine, as they probably did when they were built. Bristol has been the centre of the wine-importing business since the twelfth century and Averys, who are long-established Bristol wine merchants, still make use of medieval cellars.

Until a few years ago, Averys' extraordinary catacombs (at the bottom of Park Street, on the Council House

*Harveys' cellars, where their famous sherries were bottled until the 1960s*

side) were shrouded in mystery. One upper chamber was used for wine storage, but the rest had long lain empty. Even staff were unwilling to explore their uncharted depths, so the Temple Local History Group was asked to investigate. The Group surveyed a huge maze of cellars on several levels that run not only under Averys but out under St. George's

*One of the cellars now buried beneath Castle Park*

Road as far as the Masonic Hall and under Frog Lane as far as the Council House. Blocked entrances on both sides of Park Street make it clear that passages used to extend beneath here as well. Used by wine merchants for centuries, the cellars contain ancient "tools of the trade", such as a great stone trough for washing casks. Some highlights in the cellars' history are documented—in 1726, for example, buyers came here to view casks captured from French ships—but the full story is unclear. Exactly how old the cellars are and how far they extend beyond blocked passages is still a matter of guesswork.

Harveys' cellars, on the other hand, are the best-known in Bristol. From the entrance in Denmark Street, a labyrinth of vaults and tunnels fans out under Unity Street and Orchard Street and up as far as the Hatchet Inn. Harveys acquired these ancient cellars, along with above-

119

*Above: The spectacular cellars of the old Mansion House in Queen Square, destroyed in the Bristol Riots of 1831. The rioters drank the cellars dry—this contemporary painting depicts the aftermath!*

*Below: one of the chains of cellars which fan out under the medieval city centre from Fosters Rooms' vaults*

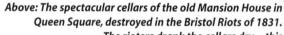

ground premises in Denmark Street, when the company was founded in 1796. The cellars remained the heart of the business until 1960. This is where the great casks were stored and the famous Bristol Milk and Bristol Cream sherries were bottled. In the 1960s Harveys moved their production facilities out of the City and a few years ago their Head Office moved from Denmark Street to Sussex. It is sad that this venerable Bristol company has left the City, but the cellars still house a Restaurant and Wine Museum which maintain the Harveys' name.

Harveys' vaults were originally the storerooms for the Hospital of St. Mark—usually known as Gaunts Hospital, because it was founded by Maurice Berkeley de Gaunt in 1220. The Berkeleys were a prominent local family and great endowers of religious and charitable institutions, including the nearby Abbey of St. Augustine (the church of which is now Bristol Cathedral). Relations between Hospital and Abbey were always strained, and the two were forever wrangling over rights to the land between them, which is now College Green. At the Dissolution of the Monasteries, Gaunts Hospital disappeared, apart from the chapel (which is now the Lord Mayor's Chapel) and the Master's House, which later became Harveys' premises. Part of this building survived until the Blitz razed it to the ground, leaving only the cellars intact.

The monks of Gaunts Hospital needed extensive cellars for their stores of wine, ale and food. The community

*Medieval cellars being used as stables in the nineteenth century*

*Paintings on pages 120-121 courtesy Sir George White*

121

was small, but it had many dependents to support. The brothers fed 100 needy citizens as well as maintaining 12 poor boys as resident scholars and providing a kind of "retirement home" for humble folk. In fact, Gaunts was a "hostel" rather than a "hospital" in the modern sense, but poverty and sickness often go together, and the good monks no doubt tended the afflicted as best they could.

The monks recognised that clean drinking water was vital for health. All the religious establishments in Bristol built complex underground conduit systems to pipe in fresh water from the springs in the surrounding hills, together with drains to take waste into the rivers. Much of this underground network still exists, and some parts are in working order.

The monks needed fresh water not only for drinking, but also for washing. The Middle Ages were not as dirty as is sometimes supposed, and in sanitation —as in everything else—the monasteries led the way. Unlike St. Agnes (who considered washing a vanity and was proud to die having never indulged in it), most religious orders placed cleanliness next to godliness. They had strict cleansing routines: hand-washing before and after meals, foot-washing on Saturdays, head-shaving every three weeks and full baths several times a year. Well-behaved brethren had warm baths, but any who were troubled by "worldly thoughts" might be prescribed a cold dip. The rigid monastic timetable even laid down set times for going to the lavatory, and every community would have a "necessary house" with long rows

*Part of Temple Pipe, hollowed out of the whole trunk of an elm tree, unearthed in the 1920s*

of
seats to
accommodate
the throng, and a
stream or drain
running underneath it.
The drain recently excavated
under St. Augustine's Abbey
(the Cathedral) seems to have
served the kitchens and lavatories,
and to have been placed below the
conduit outlet, so that it could be
vigorously flushed from time to time.

Many of the sophisticated fresh
water conduit systems that Bristol's
monks and friars built to service their
cleanly habits still run beside the gas
pipes and electric cables under modern
Bristol. The best-known of these systems
is St. John's Conduit, which still brings
spring water down from the top of Park
Street to the Church of St. John on the
Wall in Nelson Street, where it pours out
of the mouth of a stone lion's head set
into an arch in the wall. This conduit was
built in 1275 to supply the Carmelite
Friary which stood on the site of the
Colston Hall, and a branch pipe was
added in 1376 to supply St. John's.

St. John's Conduit is fed by two
springs, one under Berkeley Square and
another under the pavement outside
Blackwell's bookshop at the top of Park
Street. You can trace the course of the
conduit down Park Street via marker
stones set into the pavement. The water
itself flows through a fairly small pipe,
but this passes through impressive
masonry tunnels, large enough for men
to walk through and repair the system
whenever necessary. There are a number
of cisterns and tanks along the length of

the
conduit—one
big enough to hold
a double-decker bus. St.
John's Conduit has served
the people of Bristol faithfully,
and during the Blitz it came to the
rescue more than once. Fire-fighters
used the cisterns to douse blazing Park
Street, and for a while St. John's fountain
was the only source of fresh drinking
water in the devastated City Centre.

Sadly, bombing did not leave all the
medieval conduits unscathed. Redcliffe
Pipe, which was laid from a spring in
Knowle to St. Mary Redcliffe in 1190,
flowed unchecked until 1941, and the
outlet (an inter-war replacement of the
original) can still be seen at the corner of
Redcliffe Hill and Colston Parade. This
spout is now dry because of bomb
damage in the lower sections of the pipe,
but the upstream part still flows as far as

**Raven's Well, the source of Temple Pipe**

Whatever they did with the water, Redcliffe people have always had a special affection for their ancient conduit, and to this day they trace its whole length on an annual Pipe Walk—a very jolly event which entails "bumping" participants on the conduit's marker stones.

*Above: St. John's Conduit, showing one of the small cisterns along the route*
*Below right: The outlet of St. John's Conduit at St John on the Wall*

Victoria Park in Windmill Hill. The stream now emerges here and flows into a beautiful water maze, built in 1984 to a design based on a roof boss in St. Mary Redcliffe.

The clerics who built Redcliffe Pipe shared the water with their parishioners, and even provided a branch pipe to supply the parish of St. Thomas (near Bristol Bridge). Many religious orders were equally generous. People collected the water from public fountains and most would have used it for drinking and cooking, but those with enough money and manpower to collect and heat sufficient water enjoyed baths. Many well-to-do folk possessed a wooden bathtub—rather like a huge barrel, often padded inside with linen. In this, the whole family and their guests bathed naked together. Many medieval pictures show them happily soaking, with a meal laid on a tray across the bath and musicians to entertain the party.

*Above: The outlet of Redcliffe Pipe, near St. Mary's, which is now dry*
*Below right: The Redcliffe water maze in Victoria Park, Windmill Hill*

was from Quay Pipe, they say, that John Cabot filled up water casks to load on to his tiny ship, The Matthew, before setting sail for the New World. Quay Pipe still brings spring water to the centre of the City, but as the outlet was dismantled in the 1930s, it now flows away into the Frome.

The outlets of most of the conduits were originally embellished with a stone water fountain or "castellette". Quay Pipe had a particularly fine one, carved with a head of Momus, the god of laughter. This would have been especially appropriate in the eighteenth century, when the Quay Pipe ran with wine on coronation days.

One of Bristol's most famous landmarks—the statue of Neptune which now stands in the middle of the Centre—used to crown the castellette of Temple Pipe. This conduit was laid in 1366 to

St. John's Conduit and Redcliffe Pipe are the best preserved of the medieval conduits, but there are substantial remains of many more. Gaunts Hospital, St. Augustine's Abbey and all the other religious communities had fresh water piped to them from the hills around Bristol. Most built their own conduits, but some were granted branch pipes (known as "feathers", because they were only supposed to be big enough to accommodate a goose quill) from neighbouring systems.

Quay Pipe—the longest of all the conduits—was not built by churchmen at all, but by the City. It piped water all the way from a spring near the Boiling Well in Ashley Down, to the quayside near St. Stephen's Church. It was built in 1376 to service the booming city docks, and has a special place in the history of Bristol. It

125

supply the Friary at Temple Gate and Temple Church, with a later extension to a public fountain in Temple Street. Neptune was erected over this last outlet in the 1720s—although he has been 'moved several times before reaching his present home.

A century ago, Temple Pipe was severed by a new railway line and its outlet can no longer be traced, but its source—Raven's Well—can still be found under the "Three Lamps" signpost at Totterdown. A narrow entrance leads down into a maze of underground tunnels and reservoirs which collect the water from several springs. On the walls, the marks of the friars' pickaxes look as if they were made yesterday, and soot still coats the niches where they rested their candles. Another extraordinary relic of Temple Pipe was unearthed in the 1920s, when workmen discovered a huge wooden pipe, hollowed out of the complete trunk of an elm tree. This

probably dates from the conduit's early years, before lead piping was laid.

Over the last 20 years, some exciting discoveries in the Jacob's Wells area have revealed yet more of Bristol's ancient water system. It all began when a local householder noticed that when snow fell, it always melted first on one particular flagstone outside his house in Jacob's Wells Road. He decided to dig it up, and found a warm spring, flowing through a medieval stone-arched tunnel. This is at the head of a major conduit system which took water from several springs in the Jacob's Wells area down Brandon Hill to St. Augustine's Abbey and Gaunts Hospital.

In 1986, Mr. John Martelette made an even more startling discovery. Whilst demolishing a workshop at the junction of Jacob's Wells Road and Constitution Hill, he came across something which looked like an old fireplace, but was the entrance to a waterlogged, underground chamber. Fortunately, the Temple Local History Group recognised its significance and oversaw an excavation. When the debris was cleared (including hundreds of batteries from the police bicycles which used to be stored hereabouts!), a spring of tepid water was found to gush into the chamber from a fissure in the rock. Steps lead down into the pool, and on the lintel above is carved the Hebrew word "Sochalim" ("Flowing"). This is the oldest-

*The discovery of the Mikveh at Jacob's Wells*

known Hebrew inscription in Europe, dating from the eleventh or early twelfth century. Mr. Martelette had uncovered the medieval Jewish ritual bath, or Mikveh, which probably gave Jacob's Wells its name.

In the Middle Ages, Jews were largely restricted to dealing in finance (a matter so sordid that Christians were forbidden to soil their hands with it), and as an important commercial centre, Bristol had a substantial Jewish community. However, all Jews were expelled from England in 1290, so the Mikveh has probably lain neglected for 700 years, although the spring water continued to be used, and at one time supplied the public bath houses in Jacob's Wells Road. The Mikveh site has just been

*Bumping the marker stones on the Redcliffe Pipe Walk!*

listed, and further excavation is likely in the near future.

Local archaeologists and historians continue to unearth fascinating underground evidence of medieval Bristol. In the light of each new discovery, it is becoming increasingly obvious that, far from being the "Dark Ages", this was one of the most vigorous and exciting periods in the City's history.

## access information medieval cellars

### Harveys Wine Museum:

Harveys Wine Museum is not open to casual visitors, but group tours and tastings can be arranged: ring 0117 9275036. Diners at Harveys Restaurant also have access to the Wine Museum and cellar complex.

### Other Cellars:

At almost any time you can eat or drink in ancient cellars at Il Molino, Markwicks or many of the other bars and restaurants in Small Street, Corn Street and the surrounding area.

# Thanks...

Many people have helped in the preparation of this book. We would particularly like to thank David Harrison for his constant encouragement and support. Also Julian Lea-Jones, the Temple Local History Group and Bristol Historical Research for access to their original research.

## Special thanks also to:

Hattie Appleby
Mrs. G. Barlow
Anthony Beeson
Sue Bishop
Jonathan Brett
Bristol City Council
Bristol Industrial Museum
Alan Bryant
Nick Buller
City of Bristol Museum and Art Gallery
City of Bristol Records Office
Roger Clark
Combe Down Stone Mines Project
Nick Cripps
Peter Davey
Sophia Davies and family
Oliver Deardon
Mo Duery
Julia Elliot
The Environment Agency
David Eveleigh
Peter Flemming
Goldney Hall Warden and staff
Les Good
Simon Goodman
Alan Gray
Gerald Hart
Lu Hersey

Helen Irving
Andy King
Kingswood Heritage Museum
Living Easton
Nick McCamley
Jim McNeill
Stephen and Judy Markwick
Annie Mason
Christine Molan
Graham Mullan
Doug Northcott
Richard Poole
Prior Park College
John Rich
Rosemary Simmons
Marilyn Smith
Sheena Stoddard
Mr. M.J. Tozer
Mrs. F. Tudgey
Wendy and Jim Warrillow
Wessex Water
Sir George White

The Last Word